WHAT OTHERS SAY ABOUT
THE BIBLE STUDY TEACHER'S GUIDE

... the book comes out of "the trenches" and not from some isolated ivory tower. The author has grown in her own experience of Bible study and teaching, and she graciously shares with us some of what she has learned ... the author enjoys what God has called her to do, and that enjoyment shows in what she has written.

—Dr. Warren Wiersbe
author and Bible teacher

Beverly gets it! Bible teaching is more than transferring content from mind through mouth to the masses. It is about "iron sharpening iron"; about life linking with life; it's sharing God's rich truth from one heart to another. This guide will give you a wealth of ideas relating to content and technique with valuable insight from experienced teachers, all of which are vital. But this book will also challenge your soul, query your passion, and stir your heart to reach real people as you share the life-changing message of Christ ... and herein lies its greatest strength. Read to be informed and inflamed!

—Dr. Don Denyes
Senior Pastor
South Church, Lansing, Michigan

VanKampen's book gets to the point. It teaches teachers how to teach. No more boring presentations, sleepy students, or forgotten lessons. Teachers will love this book. Their students will love them for reading it.

—Dr. Rex Rogers, President
Cornerstone University

Many books on teaching the Bible focus on how you can help the Bible "come alive." Here is a resource that helps you come alive to the Bible. The problem is not with the Bible. The problem is with us. Beverly Van Kampen awakens me to teach the Living Word.

—Dr. Leonard Sweet
Drew University, George Fox University
www.wikiletics.com

Here is a practical book that helps all of us to be more effective at our calling, namely, to teach with clarity and conviction. The author keeps in mind that teaching is not merely intended to communicate content, but to change lives!

—Dr. Erwin W. Lutzer
Senior Pastor
The Moody Church

Beverly Van Kampen and I have partnered in ministry for the past eight years and it has been quite an adventure. Beverly brings to a serious subject—teaching the Bible—a lightness, quick wit, and sharp sense of humor that reflect Jesus, who encouraged his followers to celebrate life and lighten up. Beverly is able to do this since she has a gift for thorough research, great organization of material, a love for the written word, the Bible, the Word made flesh, Jesus, and a love for her students, of whom I am one.

—Margery Lembke
Prayer Coordinator
Lakeshore Lutheran Fellowship Church, Spring Lake, Michigan

Beverly Van Kampen has the gift of teaching. She has a unique ability to make a complex subject understandable, engaging, and intensely practical. Anyone who teaches the Bible, whether in a small group, a Sunday School gathering, an academic classroom, or a Sunday pulpit, will discover transformational help here. Through her extensive interviews, Beverly has tapped into a rich vein of "you-can-use-this-now" material. Read it! Those whom you teach will be glad you did.

—Dr. Bill Rudd, Senior Pastor
Calvary Church, Fruitport, Michigan

The Bible Study Teacher's Guide is chock full of smart advice that will help Bible teachers at all levels and in all contexts. Beverly Van Kampen offers valuable guidance for every aspect of the craft, from preparing lessons to leading discussions to one-on-one mentoring. Here the wisdom of many books is packed into a single volume.

—Dr. James S. Spiegel
Professor of Philosophy
Taylor University
and author of *How to be Good in a World Gone Bad*

Has God called you to a ministry of teaching? How do you discover that calling? And if he has called you, how do you "get ready" to teach? In this wonderfully practical book, author Beverly Van Kampen gives direction, encouragement, biblical instruction, and expert advice and examples of both how to prepare to teach and, perhaps most importantly, what God wants to do in the teacher's life as she searches the Scriptures to know the mind and heart of God. As a life-long learner, I found great wisdom and fresh insights into both the joy of teaching and the responsibilities of preparing to teach. This will be a treasured resource in my library.

—Dr. Ronald P. Mahurin
Vice President
Council for Christian Colleges and Universities

I like it . . . a lot! Here's why. First, it is refreshingly practical, offering hope, help, and confidence to the non-seminary trained "person in the pew" who may be called on to teach somewhere in the church or its related ministries. We *need* these people both to be used and to be empowered. Secondly, I see passion! Bev's personal passion for the Word of God and her passion for getting that word into the hands of the people "who will be able to teach others also" are seen throughout. That's exciting to me. Like I said, "I like it!" And you will, too.

—Rev. William Dondit
Minister with 42 years pastoral experience

THE
BIBLE
STUDY
TEACHER'S
GUIDE

THE
BIBLE
STUDY
TEACHER'S
GUIDE

BY

BEVERLY VAN KAMPEN

FOREWORD

DR. WARREN W. WIERSBE

FaithWalk
PUBLISHING
Grand Haven, Michigan

Published by FaithWalk Publishing
333 Jackson Street, Grand Haven, Michigan 49417
faithwalkpub.com

Printed in the United States of America

11 10 09 08 07 06   7 6 5 4 3 2 1

Library of Congress Cataloging-in-Publication Data

Van Kampen, Beverly.
  The Bible study teacher's guide / Beverly Van Kampen ; foreword by
    Warren W. Wiersbe.
    p. cm.
  Includes bibliographical references.
  ISBN-13: 978-1-932902-63-1 (pbk. : alk. paper)
  ISBN-10: 1-932902-63-5 (pbk. : alk. paper)
  1. Bible—Study and teaching. I. Title.
  BS600.3.K36 2006
  220.071—dc22

                    2006020534

DEDICATION

This book is dedicated to the women of God's Word who call themselves the Scripture Sisters and meet to study together on Saturday mornings at Lakeshore Lutheran Church in Spring Lake, Michigan: Beth Bentz, Nataly Berckmann, Paulette Boeger, Gloria Bouchard, Patty Chapman, Grace Cherette, Lois Eich, Mary Jo Galetto, Gail Gimborys, Karen Golden, Eva Gronevelt, Deanne Hannibal, Marcia Haslick, Eilene Kane, Carol McFall, Carol Shake, Sandy Toppen, Deb Teuling, Connie Tomhave, Sally Urso, and Louann Werksma.

And, then, a very special dedication goes to my partner in ministry, Margery Lembke, who constantly lifts me and the Bible teaching to our Lord and who leads the entire class in meaningful and effective times of prayer together.

The Scripture Sisters class has been my laboratory for learning how to teach the Bible. These students have worked beside me in digging out the truths of God's message to us, they have borne with my experimentation in teaching styles, and they have enthusiastically supported me as their friend and guide. A teacher without students is just a noisemaker. These women have allowed the Spirit to imbue the noise with meaning.

CONTENTS

FOREWORD

I enjoyed reading this book for several reasons.

To begin with, the book comes out of "the trenches" and not from some isolated ivory tower. The author has grown in her own experience of Bible study and teaching, and she graciously shares with us some of what she has learned. I'm a great fan of "This-is-what-I-learned" books. It takes humility and honesty to write them, and she has succeeded admirably.

Second, she doesn't think she knows it all yet, so she shares with us what other Bible teachers say, and that encourages me. We must learn from each other, and her quotes from other teachers of the Word are very valuable. I thank her and I thank them for handing us these nuggets of truth.

Third, the emphasis is on communicating the Word so that people can understand it and experience more of what God has for them. God forbid that we should so teach the Bible that *we* become "important" and try to get people to follow us! The emphasis is on making disciples of Jesus Christ and relating our students to him.

Finally, the author enjoys what God has called her to do, and that enjoyment shows in what she has written. It's been my privilege to teach the Word of God for more than fifty years and to write commentaries on every book of the Bible. It was work—but it was joy, and it still is! Bible teaching isn't a fatal epidemic; it's a joyful contagion, and we want others to share in the enjoyment and the enrichment of loving, learning, and living God's Word.

—Warren W. Wiersbe
Author and Bible Teacher

INTRODUCTION

If you are a Bible teacher and want to learn how to improve your skills and bring more effectiveness to your teaching, this book is for you.

If you are thinking about beginning to teach the Bible because there is a nagging sense in the back of your mind that God really wants you to share with others what you are learning about him and his Word, this book will help you to lead and teach with confidence.

If you have been asked by leaders in your church to teach a Bible study and you just don't know if you are qualified or equipped to do so, this book will help you answer that question with more certainty.

If you love to study the Bible, chances are that you will someday be called upon to teach it to others. That's just the way God works. Jesus came as the perfect model to teach a few who were then sent out to teach others who would teach still others until the whole world would know who Jesus was, why he came, and what he accomplished for us. He has not changed that plan.

As for me, I was involved as a teen in Bible studies, Bible quizzing, and contests where I memorized great chunks of Scripture and began to build a store of Bible knowledge that would provide a foundation of learning on which I would later base more formal study of the Bible during my college years. When my daughters were young, I worked only part time and was able to use some of my available time to mentor a young woman who had recently become a Christian and to teach several women's Bible study groups through the years. God rewarded those teaching ventures with positive feedback and changed lives. It was fun and exciting to see what God did with the time and effort that I gave him.

Life threw me some curves, though, and it became necessary for me to return full-time to the workforce. A divorce during this period of time caused me to lay aside my desire to teach, knowing that God needed to work with me in emotional and spiritual healing before I could stand in front of a class again with confidence and joy. I was well aware that that day might never come again. The calling at this point was more of a taste. I knew that I liked to study God's Word and that

I enjoyed teaching it. I knew that my teaching had been spiritually beneficial to several of those who studied with me. But teaching was set aside for me, and I assumed that the setting aside could be forever. God had his own plans for me.

I made a career in investment real estate, learning the trade at one company and then becoming part of a start-up operation where I stayed for twenty years, working as the company grew from two of us to more than seventy-five employees. It was a fast paced, high pressured business, but one which gave me great personal reward. I loved the business world, the people I worked with, and the satisfaction of seeing fairly significant real estate projects completed and put to use. But, as much as I loved the commercial world, I began to sense that God had something other than business in mind for me.

In May of 2000, my friend Marge Lembke and I spent a weekend in silent retreat at a Jesuit monastery about 150 miles from our hometown. Our rooms were austere (we called them "cells"), but clean and quiet. I had a single bed, a desk and chair, a toilet and sink. The only books I brought with me were my Bible and a notebook. I had come to meet with God, to realize in a new way his presence, and to listen for any direction that he might want to give me. Friday evening to Sunday afternoon I spent in silent introspection and in contemplation of God and his Word. The women attending the retreat did not speak to one another, although we shared silent meals and worship times together.

Just before we left on Sunday afternoon, God spoke clearly to my heart. No audible voice, no writing in the sky, but, nevertheless, clear instruction. He told me I was to teach women who would come to me, and I was to write. I knew that in order to do so effectively, I needed to begin to cut back on the hours I devoted to the world of real estate development. I had mixed emotions about that because I loved my work, but soon after returning home from the retreat, I was able to arrange to cut my working hours to four days a week and, shortly thereafter, to three.

I was really quite comfortable with the fact that God had told me to teach women who would come to me. That meant that I did not have to go out and find them. What were the chances of their finding me? In fact, I recently had begun to lead a women's Bible study group at the local Wesleyan Church where I was a member. Maybe that was what God had in mind when he gave me his "teach" message.

But, just a few days after the retreat, Marge received a call from Connie, a woman in her home church, a Lutheran congregation just a couple of miles from my home. Connie asked Marge if there was any way to re-start the Saturday morning Bible study that had once met at their church. Connie was hungry and wanted to learn more of God and his Word. Marge said, "I think I know just the person," and gave me a call.

I had not expected God to act so quickly. But he had called me to teach, had told me to teach women who would come to me, and, believe it or not, they began to come. I still lead that particular study on Saturday mornings, and women of various denominations and walks of life have come in to join us. God's blessing has been evident in the lives of these dear women as they have faithfully pursued a study of the Bible week after week. This group is my laboratory for nearly everything that I write and teach. They cheer me on and they challenge my thinking.

There was more. After about three years of writing, I was able to publish a devotional book. In addition, by then, I had coauthored a book on life lessons with a retired business executive and, a year later, had submitted a second devotional book to my publisher. The writing was moving along and I had a desire to devote more time to it.

Teaching opportunities were there, too, including women's retreats, some Sunday morning and evening classes in various churches, and an occasional opportunity to address a special interest group. By August of 2005, I withdrew from the company where I had worked for so many years, and, at that time, indicated to my employers that I would be able to provide consulting services for the firm but only after a complete break from the business world for sixty days.

I committed that sixty days, the months of September and October that year, to seeking God's specific direction for this new phase of my life when I would be less encumbered by the workplace and freer to pursue the gifts he had given. Would there be more writing? Would there be more teaching? Or would God's call on my life be expanded to include something other than these two things? I explored several possibilities, including a staff position in a local church, but nothing clicked as I put the opportunities in front of God for direction.

There was, however, a "distraction" to spending uninterrupted time in seeking the face of God. In August, my 79-year old, always healthy father was diagnosed with an artery blockage and had open heart surgery to complete a single bypass. He bounced back quickly and, by the end of September, was even able to play a little bit of tennis. Little did I know how much his health would relate to my calling to teach.

My dad had taught the Bible for many years. He loved teaching anyone who would listen—teens and adults mostly. He led Sunday School classes and men's Bible studies consistently through the years, cutting back only as age began to catch up with him and stepping aside to give the younger guys a chance.

My dad also was a carpenter. On September 1, just a few weeks after his surgery, my parents moved from their home of forty years to a smaller, easier-to-manage condominium a few miles away. On the day after their move, I returned to their old house to finish the cleaning and, in that process, did a final walk-through to make sure we had not left anything behind. We had, in fact, missed something.

When I went to a side room in the basement, I found a wooden tabletop lectern that Dad had been building. It wasn't even finished yet—not sanded or painted—but there it was in the middle of the room. How in the world had the basement packers not seen it? I could not walk away from it. The teacher's heart in me recognized it at once as a legacy that my dad was leaving for me. How prophetic that sense was to become just a few short weeks later. For the moment, however, I simply took the lectern home and stored it in *my* basement.

On the evening of October 2, my mother called to say that Dad had experienced chest pain after a short walk. My husband Warren and I rushed to their house and insisted on taking Dad to the emergency room. To condense the story, let me simply say that he spent the next ten days in the intensive care unit at a local hospital. He underwent several procedures, including a second open heart surgery that was not successful. He was alert and with us for several more days, but passed from this earth into the arms of Jesus on October 11.

On his final day of earthly life, Dad could not respond verbally, but he responded with his eyes and eyebrows. I talked to him about his Bible teaching through the years (eyebrows went up in acknowledgment) and about the lives he had touched by using that gift. I went on to tell him that I was doing that now; I was taking up the responsibility where he had left off. He smiled with his eyes. Then I told him about the lectern I had found and that I was going to use it to teach the Bible. He winked at me. This happened just an hour or two before he fell deeply to sleep, never to awaken to his old life again.

A few days later (and still in my sixty days of focus), I was again seeking God's face and his clear direction in my life. I had taken a few days from my prescribed Bible readings in light of the emotional trauma I had suffered over the previous two weeks. Instead, I had been reading scriptural passages of comfort and peace. Now I asked God what he wanted me to read. I thought maybe something in John, or a psalm, but he clearly laid on my heart the book of II Timothy. As I read, I realized I was reading the words of Paul the Apostle as he was preparing to leave this world. He wanted to pass on the responsibility of the spreading of the Gospel and the building up of churches to his protégé, young Timothy. This was a highly significant book because these were among Paul's last words.

As I read them, it was as if each command was for me:

> Fan into flame the gift of God (1:6)
> Do not be ashamed to testify (1:8)
> Follow the pattern of sound teaching you have learned
> (1:5 and 3:14–15, paraphrased).
> Guard the deposit entrusted to you (1:14).
> Remind, warn (2:14).
> Don't quarrel over words (2:14 and 2:23–24, paraphrased).
> Correctly handle the word of truth (2:15, paraphrased).
> Gently instruct (2:25).
> Continue in what you have learned (3:14).
> Be prepared always (4:2, paraphrased).

There were more commands, but I am sure by now you understand what I am saying. The words of this book came alive. It seemed that I was their target. It was as if each sentence were highlighted. God used the time I had set aside for seeking his direction as a time to share my earthly father's last days; but, in doing so, also to prepare me for a reiteration of the calling on my life to teach his Word.

When God gave me the message of II Timothy, my sixty days of seeking were not quite up, but I knew at that moment that I had my answer. FaithWalk Publishing had already asked that I consider writing the book you are now reading, a book to help laity teach the Bible with more confidence and effectiveness. That book request, to me, correlated directly with Paul's instructions to Timothy to pass on what he had learned to others so that they could carry on the work. My dad passed the baton to me, and I am now running the race with you. What I have learned and what I have been able to glean from other Bible teachers, I am giving to you so that God's Word can come alive in your hands, and the desire you have for teaching about him will grow into a burning passion that will be used by the Spirit to change lives.

In one sense, we are all teachers. There are those who learn from us whether we intend them to or not. In another sense, there are some of us for whom teaching is a special gift, a calling, and a passion. Our need to teach grows out of our love for learning. Our teaching is intentional, not accidental.

That is the case for me. I love to learn and I have found that, as I soak in knowledge and understanding, the greatest satisfaction comes in sharing those things with someone else. In my early adult life, I put this into practice by teaching English in a public high school and teaching in an English-speaking middle school in Central America many years ago. I also put my love for teaching into practice in the business arena as opportunities to teach aspects of the trade to others arose during my twenty-some years in real estate development.

By far the most satisfying teaching I have done, however, has been teaching the Bible. I am not seminary trained, but I have studied the Bible all my life, including some formal training during college years. The Bible is a fascinating book for me because of its unending depth, its intellectual challenges, its historical accounts, its relational wisdom, and its connection to the mind and heart of God. So I read it. I peruse commentaries. I read books by authors who have studied it more thoroughly than I. I absorb it, ponder it, interact with it, and allow it to sink into the depths of my being. Once I do all that, I just have to share with someone else what I have taken in.

Most of my teaching has been in small group Bible studies of women and/or couples or in Sunday School classes of young adults or teens. So, this book is written for those of you who are in similar situations: teaching Sunday School, leading group discussions, hosting the study of a Christian book, mentoring an individual, or creating and presenting your own study materials directly from the Bible.

My teaching experience is very limited in comparison with many others in this world. So, it was my privilege in the preparation for writing this book to interview a number of the master teachers who have taught formally and informally for many years—in universities, in public schools, and in churches. Those who contributed their wisdom and experience to this teacher's guide are as follows:

Warren Wiersbe	Author, radio teacher, pastor
Erwin W. Lutzer	Pastor, author, radio teacher
Ravi Zacharias	Apologist, author, international evangelist
Ronald Mahurin	Vice President of the Council of Christian Colleges and Universities, author, former professor
Rex Rogers	College president
William Rudd	Pastor, college board trustee
Don Denyes	Associate seminary professor, pastor
Jo Kadlecek	Author, teacher
Nataly Berckmann	Art teacher, public schools
Phyllis Nye	Speech teacher, public schools
Tamara Rosier	Pedagogy professor
Kathleen O. Sindorf	Communications professor
William Dondit	Pastor, teacher

Their insights are quoted throughout each chapter, and I know you will enjoy peeking into the hearts and minds of some of our brightest and best Christian teachers. I give special thanks to all of them for their willingness to participate in this project and, particularly, to Dr. Warren Wiersbe for writing the Foreword to this book. It was a delight to talk to these men and women, who not only teach well, but take joy in sharing what they have learned about the craft with those of us who are not as far along in our practice of the great gift of teaching. Their enthusiasm and encouragement were truly inspiring.

I trust that the instruction and insight provided in each chapter will give you practical help as you prepare to engage your students and, even more, that it will encourage you to keep moving forward in your own learning, in your walk with Jesus as our Master Teacher, and in your effectiveness in sharing the message of God's Word with all who are willing to listen and learn.

Beverly Van Kampen
2006

ONE

WHEN TEACHING AND PASSION INTERSECT

Do you want the best and most wonderful gifts God has given you to decay, spent on your own self? Or do you want them to be set free to come into their own as you link your profoundest abilities with your neighbor's need and the glory of God? Listen to Jesus of Nazareth; answer his call.

—Os Guinness in *The Call*

After reading this chapter, you will better understand:

- [ ] What it means to be called to teach.
- [ ] How such a calling may change and grow over time.
- [ ] How you can test your calling by experience.
- [ ] How the prophet Samuel's call to ministry serves as a biblical model for us.

Teaching without a calling is like trying to climb a mountain in ballet slippers. The desire is real, the inviting mountain peak is in front of us, but it's hard to get there. Pretty soon, we lose our footing, our feet begin to hurt, and we give up in discouragement. If we are teaching the Bible without having been called by God to do so, we may be able to communicate facts and truths, but passion and power will be the missing ingredients. Both are automatic if the calling is there. And a passionate teacher will make a great deal more progress in life-changing ministry than one who is simply putting in the time.

For many teachers of the Bible, their "calling" was more likely a phone call from a pastor or the Christian education director pleading with them to take on the high school Bible class because no one else would do it. Unless God confirms such a request, run! There is no worse place to be than in a position of leadership in the church for which you are not called and prepared by God. On the other hand, there is no better place to be than in the center of God's will, doing what he has created us to do, experiencing the power and understanding that only the Holy Spirit can give, and sensing that God is reaching other people through us. If God is calling, don't miss it!

Then, how do we know if we are called to teach? A calling to teach might be described as God singling you out and creating in your heart a desire to learn of him, his ways, and his Word, and then to communicate that learning to others. Calling may not happen in one burst of revelation. More likely it will begin with a nudge—simply a sense of wanting to know more of God. It will then grow into a stronger and stronger desire to share with other people what is being learned. And, eventually, you know beyond any doubt that teaching is what you were created to do. Teaching is what drives your learning. Teaching is what energizes you and inspires you to inspire others. Teaching, at that point, has become your calling.

My own calling to teach did, as I described in the Introduction, occur in stages, unfolding over time as I became more and more open to God's direction in my life. I had been educated as a high school English teacher and was able to put my teaching skills to work in education and business settings, but I found my greatest satisfaction in teaching the Bible to anyone anywhere who would listen to me. The more I taught, the more God confirmed in the very center of my being that this was what he had had in mind for me to do all along. As I studied the Bible, realized the need for spiritual knowledge in the lives of those around me, and listened to the gentle urgings of the Holy Spirit, God's calling on my life became clearer and clearer. And I believe that I have not seen it all yet. The calling and the practice of it unfold day by day and, as long as I am responsive to God's leading, I believe it will continue to unfold.

My goal is to share with you what I have learned about how to teach and write in ways that will be heard and read. But there are many highly qualified Christian teachers in our world who are much more advanced in this knowledge than I am. Many of them, including some with internationally known ministries, have graciously contributed thoughts and experiences that are incorporated into this book (see Introduction for complete list). Their unique insights will provide us welcome instruction in the fine art of teaching the principles of God's Word to those who are eager to hear. The wealth of experience and understanding provided by these men and women, whom I refer to in this text as *master teachers*, has been incorporated throughout each chapter.

As we are going to discuss in this chapter various ways by which God calls his people into teaching, this is a good place for sharing with you some of ways these master teachers experienced God's calling on their lives. You will notice that each call is as different as the individual whom God directs. Yet there are some commonalities that help each of us to have a better sense of God's means of guiding our steps and our service to him. As I give you their stories, I introduce these master teachers to you so that you will recognize them when you encounter them again throughout the reading.

Early on in my life I wanted to be a preacher, not so much a teacher. It was later when I went to Bible school and seminary that I wanted to be like my profs, so I took an interest in teaching. I was about to become a professor in a Bible college or seminary when God guided me back to the preaching ministry. But I have never lost my love of teaching.

—Dr. Erwin Lutzer

Dr. Lutzer is the senior pastor of The Moody Church in Chicago, where he has preached and taught for more than twenty-five years. In addition, he is the bestselling author of many books and the Bible teacher on a daily international radio program entitled *Running to Win* as well the weekly *Moody Church Hour*.

I don't know if my call to teach ever came as a revelation. It was more a question of what I felt really compelled to do. Desire often translates into gifting. If we take delight in the Lord, he will give us the desires of our heart. When we delight in him, he instills in our hearts our true desires and then fulfills them. I grew up wanting to teach. Teaching is what I always thought I would be doing.

— Jo Kadlecek

Ms. Kadlecek is a freelance writer and communications teacher who lives in New Jersey. She has taught at both high school and college levels, presently specializing in teaching of writing at conferences and workshops. She has written several books, with her newest release entitled *Desperate Women of the Bible: Lessons on Passion from the Gospels*.

At about age 14, I despised speaking in public. I liked theological studies, but I knew I would never want to be a teacher. In Youth for Christ, though, we were forced to give testimonies. The first time I had to do it, I was almost physically ill. But I gave my testimony and the reaction was so positive that, from that point on, people were encouraging me to go into ministry. I began praying with peers who were of the same mind concerning the possibility of full-time ministry. During college I led a Bible study, and God blessed my efforts. But I struggled because I didn't want to go into ministry just because some of my friends were doing it. One time the struggle continued into the night and Isaiah 40 came to mind about the voice crying in the wilderness. It was as if God clearly said to me, "I want you to be that voice." From that time on, I took every opportunity I had to speak and to teach.

—Dr. Don Denyes

Dr. Denyes is the senior pastor of South Church in Lansing, Michigan, and associate professor of homiletics at Grand Rapids Seminary.

I didn't realize the gift God had given me until I put it into practice.   *

—Phyllis Nye

Ms. Nye is a Florida resident with thirty-four years of experience in teaching middle school speech, drama, and English in public schools.

I knew that I wanted to teach long before I understood the concept of giftedness. Growing up, the pastor's wife was our youth leader. When I was about twelve years old, she had each of us bring in a talk or a story or something to share with the group. I preached from Matthew 7:7–8 and still have the notes. It was amazing how good it felt! I knew I wanted to do it again.

— Dr. Bill Rudd

Dr. Rudd is the senior pastor of Calvary Church in Fruitport, Michigan, a congregation he has served for more than twenty-five years. In addition, he is an adjunct professor at Grand Rapids Seminary and serves on the Board of Trustees and Academic Committee of Cedarville University in Ohio.

When I was converted at the age of sixteen, I experienced a great hunger for the Word and began to read and study my Bible and to use Bible commentaries. In my church, I was given opportunities to teach in Vacation Bible School and Sunday School, and others affirmed the gift ... The church I attended lost its pastor in 1950 and they asked me to fill in when they didn't have a candidate or guest speaker, and eventually they called me to pastor the church!

—Dr. Warren Wiersbe

Dr. Wiersbe is one of the evangelical world's most respected Bible teachers. He has served on the staff of Youth for Christ and has pastored a number of churches through the years. For ten years, he was the Bible teacher and general director of the *Back to the Bible* radio broadcast. He is the author of more than one hundred books, including expository outlines of the Bible and biblical commentaries.

I realized early in high school that I was able to teach, even with my peers, but I never thought of teaching as a career. There was a moment, though, when in my first year of college, my boyfriend (who is now my husband) said, "You would really make a great teacher." It seemed right; it was one of those moments when everything came together. I began to get the training I needed to develop the gift that I now recognized.

—Dr. Tamara Rosier

Dr. Rosier is an Assistant Professor of Education at Cornerstone University in Grand Rapids, Michigan. She holds a doctoral degree in pedagogy and has taught at the secondary school level and in ministry settings for many years. Dr. Rosier is also the Director of Cornerstone's Center for Excellence in Learning and Teaching and serves as the Assistant Dean of Faculty Development for the University.

I am not quite sure when exactly I sensed this was my call and gift from the Lord. There were many occasions when pastors or missionaries would say something to me after I shared my testimony. I suppose it would be fair to say that it happened over a period of time and then crystallized during a visit to Vietnam when I preached there midway through my undergraduate studies ...

—Dr. Ravi Zacharias

Dr. Zacharias is a renowned lecturer and teacher who has spoken to political and university groups worldwide. In addition, he preaches on a weekly radio program entitled *Let My People Think* and is the author of numerous books on world religions, theology, and philosophy. He heads RZIM, a ministry with offices in six countries of the world.

From these stories and from biblical example, what can we learn about the calling to teach?

- A calling may (but may not!) build on early interests and life experience.

In my case, I already had a teaching degree and experience teaching high school and middle school before entering the business world. The inborn inclinations of my heart combined with the secular education I received to prepare me for the calling that God was later to put on my life to teach his Word and his truth to those willing to listen. The same was true in the experience some of the master teachers cited on previous pages.

One of the clearest stories of calling in the Bible is the account given in I Samuel 3 of God calling Samuel, who became a prophet of truth in the land of Israel. Samuel's mother, Hannah, had given him to the work of the Lord by leaving him as a helper in the temple of God at Shiloh. So, Samuel grew up consistently exposed to the ritual of the sacrificial system and worship ceremonies in the temple and under the teaching of Eli the high priest. Coming into God's presence was familiar to him as it was a part of the very nature of his daily life as a child. God later used these early childhood experiences to make him an effective and powerful prophet and teacher throughout the land of Israel and beyond.

- A calling will be understood by a sense of direction from God through prayer and reading of Scripture.

My first real sense of calling came at a time of personal retreat, when I was immersing myself in God's Word and his presence. I believe that the sensitivity to God's direction was clearer because I had separated myself from the busyness of life in order to hear his voice. He honored my desire to know his will and direction and gave it to me clearly as a result of my willingness to seek his face. For others, as you have read, the initial call was more practical in nature.

But, Samuel's initial calling came when he was ". . . lying down in the temple of the Lord, where the ark of God was" (I Samuel 3:3). He had chosen to sleep in the vicinity of the ark, in the very presence of God himself. When we deliberately choose to be with God, I believe he is pleased. Our active seeking of him evidences the sincerity of our hearts and our true desire to serve him. It is in times like these that we are most likely to hear his specific call upon our lives.

- Obedience to a calling is optional.

What if God calls us to do something we do not want to do? It happens and, when it does, we have a choice. But I have also found that, if we obey the calling even when it doesn't sound too appealing, God will provide the desire and eagerness to do what he wants us to do. God will not force his will on us, though. If we refuse to obey his calling, we will miss out on the joy of working alongside the God of the universe in accomplishing his plan in our world. Once the calling is clear, I cannot imagine any reason not to follow it.

The prayer of my heart is that when God calls, I will listen and will eagerly obey just as the boy Samuel did. Once Samuel realized that the voice he heard as he lay in the temple was God himself, he responded, "Speak, for your servant is listening." God is willing to speak, but primarily if we are willing to listen and obey.

- A calling will be confirmed by circumstances and people around us.

In my case, a few days after I received God's message that he wanted me to teach women who would come to me, Marge called to say that Connie had asked if she knew of anyone who would teach a women's Bible study. This confirmed to me in capital letters that I had heard God correctly and that he now was testing me to see if I would be obedient to his call. I said, "yes" to Connie's request, not without some insecurity about my ability to teach effectively, but with complete confidence that God was steering me in the direction he wanted me to go.

I had reported my calling to my friend Marge; Samuel had reported his to the old priest Eli. Eli never questioned that it was God who had spoken, nor did he question the message that Samuel heard. Instead, he confirmed the call to Samuel by saying, "He is the Lord; let him do what is good in his eyes" (I Samuel 3:18).

- A calling will be confirmed by the results of our practice of it.

One way you know you are called to teach is if people learn from you. A teacher is not just someone who stands up in front and spews information. A teacher teaches. When one who is called

> *When one who is called teaches God's Word, it is released in power and lives are changed.*

teaches God's Word, it is released in power and lives are changed. If we are teaching and nothing is happening in the lives of our students, we must ask whether we are truly practicing the calling that God has for us—or we must ask if there is sin or selfishness or pride in our lives that is blocking the power of the Holy Spirit in the kingdom work that God desires to accomplish through us.

In Samuel's case, we are told, "The Lord was with Samuel as he grew up, and he let none of his words fall to the ground. And all Israel from Dan to Beersheba recognized that Samuel was attested as a prophet of the Lord" (I Samuel 3:19-20). The people recognized Samuel's calling. They knew that when he spoke, whatever he spoke about was true. Whatever he prophesied happened just as he said. Credibility was built because God had called him and that calling was evident to those who observed Samuel all through his life.

- A calling may be renewed or expanded over a lifetime.

As I have been willing to step away from full-time work in the business world—first to part-time work and finally to none at all— I believe God has expanded his calling in my life. He not only has opened up opportunities to write and to teach "women who would come to me" as in the initial calling, but through my careful study of his Word I have received a broader understanding of the role of women in the church and as a result have expanded my teaching to include men (usually as part of a couples group) as well as women.

There was a total renewal of my calling after my father left this world and I sensed that the mantle of teaching ministry that he had begun now was passed to me. As recounted in the Introduction, the teaching of II Timothy came alive to me as God continued to encourage me to follow his calling in my life without holding back. At this point, he has taken away concerns about lack of formal seminary education, about my imperfect marital history, and about my being a woman and is building in me a new freedom and passion for teaching his Word to whomever will listen to me teach or read what I write.

Again, there are parallels in Samuel's life. The history books of the Old Testament are replete with Samuel stories. He was the great prophet in Israel at the end of the time of the judges. He anointed the first king of Israel, Saul, and tried during the reign of Saul to keep the people focused on God as their true leader. When Saul failed to follow God, Samuel, at God's direction, anointed the shepherd boy, David, to be the second king of Israel. To sum it up, we are told, "The Lord continued to appear at Shiloh, and there he revealed himself to Samuel through his word" (I Samuel 3:21).

By this biblical account we know that God usually does not reach out to us just once, but he *continues* to lead those whom he has called so that they are walking in lockstep with him and so that they are providing the teaching and leadership in a way that is consistent with his perfect plan. During that process, our roles and specific responsibilities may change as we adjust to the ongoing and evolving calling of God upon our lives.

 ## Let's Review and Evaluate

Has God called you to teach?

Has he given you a passion for studying his Word so that you can share with others its transforming message?

Is he providing opportunities for you to share what you have learned?

Do others find your teaching interesting and insightful?

If so, read on. This book is written for you. When God calls us, he knows we still have rough edges. He knows that we still have a lot to learn about doing well the job he has given us. So he challenges us to begin to learn not only the Bible, but how to present it in ways that are effective in leading others to the truth.

TWO

PREPARING THE MESSENGER

Only someone who has been there, who has drunk the dregs
of our cup of pain, who has experienced the existential loneliness
and alienation of the human condition, dares whisper the name
of the Holy to our unspeakable distress.
Only that witness is credible; only that love is believable.

—Brennan Manning in *Ruthless Trust*

As you read this chapter, look for the following:

- The close relationship between the message you give and the person you are.
- How your teaching can have supernatural power.
- Why it's important to keep going even if you get discouraged.
- How you can experience joy in your teaching and your relationships.

I heard a speaker once deliver a message of love and forgiveness, and I was so captivated that I arranged to meet her a couple of weeks later to find out more. She was not quite thirty years old and had been married for several years to a man she loved but with whom she did not always see eye-to-eye. One day he did not come home from work at his usual time. As the evening wore on, she began to get very concerned and enlisted the help of family, and eventually the police, to find him. In the early morning hours, a friend found him slumped over the wheel of his pickup truck, which was parked in a remote field some miles from home. He had been shot and killed!

A subsequent investigation and trial revealed that her husband's murderer was a neighbor with whom this woman had been having an affair. An avowed Christian, her deepest secret was now splashed all over the front pages of the newspapers every day for several weeks as the investigation and ensuing trials revealed the sordid details of her secret acts. The pain in her heart was great, but she repented of her sin and accepted the forgiveness of God and the renewal of her spirit as she began to practice belonging solely and completely to him.

As the trial wore on, there were cameras in her face daily. She had to testify against the man she had thought she loved and who she now realized was emotionally unstable and dangerous. She carried the undeniable guilt of having contributed to her husband's murder.

You can imagine that, after she told this story as an introduction to her message, she had everyone in the audience on the edges of their seats. She was not a polished speaker; she did not exegete a difficult passage of Scripture, nor did she have three alliterated points. But her message—of God's love for her in spite of her sinful decisions and of the supernatural ability to forgive those who had wronged her—affected all of us as we thought of our own sinfulness and the petty issues that we tended to hold against others.

Why was her story so powerful? Partly because of its drama. But the real power, I felt, was the change that had occurred in the speaker's life as a result of having gone through this experience. The transformation was so evident and so inspiring that I kept thinking, "I want the kind of relationship with God that she has." The story of the affair and the murder would have been just another sad story and would have had no impact without her calmly radiant face and changed life.

The same is true about the effectiveness of our teaching. The impact we have on those who listen to us will be directly proportional to the impact that God's Word and his Spirit are having in our lives. There is a lot of work that goes into teaching a lesson but, as teachers, we are first learners, so our tendency is to focus on learning more and more stuff so we have more and more to say. The purpose of this chapter is to challenge us to devote commensurate time and attention on preparing ourselves to teach. In the spiritual realm, that preparation is probably more significant than the materials presented in the lesson itself.

The master teachers agree, and they share various approaches to keeping their own spiritual lives vital and their relationship with God on the growing edge. Here is what some of them have to say on this subject:

Before I leave for school in the morning, I spend time in prayer. Even while I am driving to my classroom, I am praying in order to ready myself for the day. In doing this, God reminds me of my purpose in this world and why he has given me the job of teaching. My relationship with Jesus goes with me to the classroom. My spiritual life and my teaching life are not separate worlds. I make it my goal to show God's light to everyone that I meet.

—Nataly Berckmann

Ms. Berckmann is an artist who teaches elementary children in a public school in western Michigan. She has taught for a total of twenty-three years, first in a program for migrant children, then as a reading specialist, and in most recent years as an art instructor.

Meditation on the material and prayer for the Lord's help. I ask God to fill my mind with truth, my heart with love ("speaking the truth in love" —Ephesians 4:15) and my will with power and self-control.

—Dr. Warren Wiersbe

I pray, think it through. I take a lot of bike rides because the bike allows alone time without distraction and the exercising helps the brain to work. I research and I write. I am at the point in my life where I have to write out most of my talks to ensure that I do not have blank moments. I don't want my presentation to be an academic experience. It needs to be kneaded into me so it becomes part of my experience. It it's not real to me, no one will care what I have to say. Ultimately, though, it is the Scripture that makes the difference. Hopefully, they [students] will always look at a passage differently because we have studied it together.

—Jo Kadlecek

I prepare myself spiritually for teaching through prayer, but not asking God for anything, at least not right away. I believe that prayer is primarily connecting with God, it is drawing near to God for fellowship and yieldedness. It is making the most of his presence as we learn to enjoy him and rest in his goodness.

—Dr. Erwin Lutzer

I try to remain open to God's Spirit in ways that will allow me to hear what he wants me to say. I also find that conversations with colleagues, friends, my spouse, and others can be valuable in discerning what God may want to say through my teaching. In the end, there does not seem to be any magical formula, and, depending on time and other factors, there are moments when I simply go on instinct—what I sense is needed for the moment and the audience.

—Dr. Ronald Mahurin

Dr. Mahurin is the Vice President for Professional Development and Research at the Council for Christian Colleges and Universities [CCCU] headquartered in Washington DC. He has served on the faculty at both Westmont College in Santa Barbara, California and Gordon College in Boston, Massachusetts. He is also the author and coauthor of two books on the political responsibilities of Christians.

Preparation is a constant state of mind and discipline. Speaking at a particular venue is not like preparing for exams. You must be in a preparation mode constantly. I then focus on possible questions that will come from the audience to whom that talk is presented. That helps you anticipate and defuse them beforehand. Spiritually, I prepare with a daily devotional life and offer each presentation to God before it is delivered to the people. Prayer and reflection are key.

—Dr. Ravi Zacharias

Obviously, the given is keeping your own walk with God dynamic, personal, and intimate. There is no substitute for that. Prayer and spending time in the Word are also very important. There is also no substitute for the hard work of study …

—Rev. William Dondit

Rev. Dondit has been a pastor for forty-two years in three different churches. Presently he and his wife Dee Ann are semi-retired and are living in Wheeling, Illinois.

It is my goal to develop a real and growing relationship with the Lord. I do this through a Bible reading plan and a memorization plan. By following these, I get into the Word in a way that is separate from studying for preaching or teaching. I want the Word of God to come to my heart before I preach it.

—Dr. Don Denyes

Teaching is a form of spiritual discipline because it is a sacred trust. Having to teach forces you into Scripture. You always learn more than the recipients of your teaching. I pray to be helped to communicate well.

—Dr. Rex Rogers

Dr. Rogers is the president of Cornerstone University in Grand Rapids, Michigan, a position he has held since 1991. In addition, he is the writer and speaker for a daily radio feature and is the author of three books and an ongoing newspaper column. Those publications have led to more than 150 media interviews around the nation.

For the past three years that I taught, a dear elderly lady in our church, Millie Peck, prayed for me every day. Those three years were the best teaching years of my career! When I needed spiritual support, I would call Millie and tell her the specifics of what I was troubled by or the stresses I was facing. Generally, though, I found that the spiritual preparation came when I was professionally prepared by knowing my subject and relationally prepared by knowing my students.

—Phyllis Nye

I see teaching as a responsibility, not a right. I am a servant in that classroom. That means that I want to do a good job. I pray, asking for God's blessing over each student. I pray that solid relationships will be built as I meet with my class to prepare them to teach. This is a holy time for them. I know the course content, but the spiritual preparation is essential. At the end of each semester, I feel blessed to have been able to teach. I am not in teaching for the power; instead, teaching is my offering.

—Dr. Tamara Rosier

I discipline myself not to reach for the Bible in preparing to study without first praying. I commit the study and the lesson preparation to the Lord. I don't want to be glorified myself, but I want him to speak through me. I ask him to show me things, as I study, that I would miss without his enlightenment. When I have an opportunity to teach, I try to slow down to ask "Is this what you want me to teach, Lord, now?"

—Kathleen O. Sindorf

Ms. Sindorf has spent most of her career in television producing and broadcasting, including work at the Christian Broadcasting Network (CBN) and at Channel 38 in Chicago. She recently joined the faculty of Cornerstone University after serving five years as a vice president and teacher with Kay Arthur for Precept Ministries of Chattanooga, Tennessee.

For further instruction in this essential spiritual preparation, we always can go straight to the Bible. Here is one passage that addresses these important heart issues:

> Create in me a pure heart, O God,
> and renew a steadfast spirit within me.
> Do not cast me from your presence
> or take your Holy Spirit from me.
> Restore to me the joy of your salvation
> and grant me a willing spirit, to sustain me.
> Then I will teach transgressors your ways,
> and sinners will turn back to you. (Psalm 51:10–13)

King David, the author of these words, is willing to share God's message with others, but he recognizes that there are some changes that need to occur in him before he is ready to teach anyone else. What does he ask for? Purity, steadfastness, the Holy Spirit, joy, and willingness. Once he has these characteristics, David is confident that his teaching will turn people toward God. Without them, he knows that any teaching he does will fall flat and will not produce changed lives. Only God's living Spirit can accomplish that!

Let's take a look at what David is asking for.

- A pure heart.

I used to resist going to God and asking him to reveal sin in my life. I didn't like being wrong, being bad, or being found out. Then I realized that I was treating sin in my life as a child might react when caught with his hand in the cookie jar. It's really not like that at all. Sin is not about being caught. God already knows our sinfulness. He simply waits for us to recognize it, too, so that he and we can be honest with each other about its effect in our lives and, in that honesty, God can begin to work to change us.

As I have matured in my faith, I now see confession of sin as a wonderfully freeing activity. I look forward to meeting God in the morning, asking the Holy Spirit to search me and reveal to me any sin in my life that I need to confess. Why is that now a positive experience? Because I really *like* getting cleaned up. It feels as good as taking a hot, soapy bath after getting sweaty and grubby from working in the yard all day. Getting dirty is never as much fun as we think it's going to be. Getting cleaned up is refreshing and ennobling and prepares us for a new day and a new assignment from God. I no longer avoid asking God to reveal sin. I welcome his probing light and am learning not to justify myself, but simply to agree with him when he says that something is sin. I confess it, ask for his forgiveness, and accept the cleansing that comes (I John 1:9). It feels *good*, not bad!

Another thing I have learned is that my sin never takes God by surprise. He knows my frailty, and he knows that I will sin. He does not expect perfection from me, but he does expect that I will care enough about my relationship to him that, when I do sin, I will want to come clean. I will acknowledge what I have done and ask him to bring forgiveness and cleansing into my life. Jesus died to do just that. God is all about forgiveness and restoration. We just have to be willing to agree with God that our sin blocks our relationship with him and our effectiveness in serving him.

A word of caution: Teachers can be especially vulnerable to the sin of pride. We study a lot, we probably understand more than our students do, and we receive positive feedback from those who study with us. All of that can add up to our thinking we are gifted, we are special, and God really could not get his work done without us. As my husband says, "Be careful. Pretty soon you are going to start believing all the things people say about you and then you will be pretty hard to live with!"

While the recognition of pride in our hearts is usually more subtle than that, I think it is imperative for teachers to constantly be on guard against it. We must consistently ask God to show us if there is even a seed of pride that is beginning to sprout in our lives and then root it out when he does. We will talk more about this in Chapter 8. There are other sins, too, that seem to haunt those of us who teach. Here are some to be particularly sensitive to:

Arrogance: The attitude that we have all the answers, or at least more than most, will most certainly be detected by our students. "Humble yourselves before the Lord, and he will lift you up" (James 4:10). Students are more ready to learn from a teacher who meets them on their level without talking down to them.

Insecurities: Conversely, there usually is no one harder on teachers than teachers themselves. Insecurities are the other side of the coin of pride. Feeling insecure means that we are thinking of ourselves instead of the ones we serve. We are worried about what people think, how they will react, and whether we should put on a different personality. We must be ourselves and accept ourselves as instruments in the hand of God. And he never feels insecure!

Comparisons: There are myriad Bible teachers out there, and many of them are more popular and get better results than you or I ever will. That's OK. We are to serve where God has placed us. We are to teach those he has put in our paths—and we are to do it with all the devotion and sincerity that we can give it. The rest is up to God. So we must not envy someone else's teaching style or ministry or class size. To do so is a sin that will stop us short of being effective teachers of the Bible.

Untruths: As teachers, we want to make strong points, we want to have the best stories, and we want to create the right emphases. This desire makes us prone to use exaggeration to make a point or to put a spin on a verse of Scripture or on a story we are telling. We must avoid such temptation. God will honor truth and truth alone. Our goal is to stick specifically to the message God gives without having to embellish it. The power is in the truth.

God will not use a dirty vessel. If we are not willing to confess sin that God reveals (or if we are not willing even to ask him to show us the sin in our lives), his power cannot work through us. We will be attempting to teach his Word and his holiness, but we will fail. We need his power working in us in order to produce anything of eternal value. We will not have that power if we are not thoroughly cleaned up in the bathtub of prayer, examination, and confession. It's that simple.

Flee the evil desires of youth, and pursue righteousness, faith, love and peace along with those who call on the Lord out of a pure heart. (II Timothy 2:22)

- A steadfast spirit.

This is the second characteristic David prays for. If you have taught for any length of time, I suspect you have thought about quitting at least once (or maybe once a week!). Teaching is hard work. Interrelating with students takes a lot of energy. Putting together lessons that are both captivating and insightful requires a great deal of creativity, time, and study. David asked for the ability to be steadfast, which means that he needed God-inspired strength in order to stick to it when he felt like quitting.

In many ways, good teaching is like other skills in that we get better at it the more we do it. If we quit when the going gets rough, we will never be able to develop in full the teaching gifts that God has given us. If we know that God has called us to teach, we should not stop until he clearly gives us a different direction.

But you, keep your head in all situations, endure hardship, do the work of an evangelist, discharge all the duties of your ministry. (II Timothy 4:5)

- The presence of the Holy Spirit.

David recognizes his dependence on God's Spirit. For us, too, who teach God's Word, teaching is not a job, it is a calling. The one who calls us, inspires us, empowers us, and guides us is the Holy Spirit himself. In fact, Jesus told his disciples that after he left this earth, the Holy Spirit would be their teacher. If we do it the way God intended, we are taught by the Spirit and then we turn around and teach to others what we have been taught ourselves. Great plan, isn't it?

The problem with the plan is that nothing else in the world works that way. If you see teaching as a job, you study harder, you work on your presentation skills, you choose subjects that will be of interest to your students, and you measure whether you have reached your objectives. God's way is different from our way. It is more important to God that we be sensitive to the leading, teaching, and empowering of the Holy Spirit than it is that we be eloquent or scholarly or funny or popular. If we are Holy Spirit led, our teaching will be successful in accordance with God's lesson plans, not ours.

Teaching is defined in the writings of Paul as a "spiritual gift." In other words, God does not call us to teach without gifting us with the ability to teach on a spiritual level. That gift is given through the Holy Spirit. If we truly believe that, then we acknowledge that the most important preparation we can make for our teaching is to stay connected to the Spirit and to seek his direction in what we teach and how we teach it. After we have received that guidance, we can begin the studying, the lesson planning, the presentation, and the evaluation— all under the Spirit's direction and empowerment.

Many books have been written on the guidance of the Holy Spirit (some are listed in Chapter 9), so I won't go into great detail here as to how to seek God's direction. We, simply, at this point, acknowledge that teaching without the Holy Spirit is like trying to drive a car without turning on the engine. We might look really good behind the wheel, but we won't get anywhere!

Guard the good deposit that was entrusted to you—guard it with the help of the Holy Spirit who lives in us. (II Timothy 1:14)

- Joy of salvation.

It's no fun sitting in the classroom of a gloomy teacher. Some of the very best teachers I have had were able to combine humor with some very serious material. They had a zest for life. They had developed an eternal perspective in facing whatever problems they encountered. They knew that, no matter what, God was in charge, and, because of that, they could have joy even in the midst of negative circumstances. Joy shows. It shows on our faces, in our messages, and in our voices.

David knew that he would not be an effective teacher until God had given him true joy. If we struggle with the joy factor in our lives, we may need to pray David's prayer. As someone once said, "Don't take life so seriously. You're not going to get out of it alive anyway!" So, relax, smile, enjoy your relationship with God, and have fun with the teaching assignments he gives you.

Rejoice in the Lord always. I will say it again: Rejoice! (Philippians 4:4)

- A willing spirit.

"OK, God" is a great response to anything God asks you to do. It's the right answer when he points out sin in our lives that we need to confess. It's the right answer when he asks that we step out of our comfort zones to do something we have never tried before. As I read through Scripture, I sometimes find a passage that I don't quite understand or that seems to be telling me something I am not sure I want to agree with. I read it until I can say, "OK, God." He and I know that my saying those words means that, even if I don't have all the answers, even if I don't have complete understanding, even if I can't figure out how he will accomplish what he is asking me to do, I am willing to accept what he says as truth and to do what he directs me to do.

I invite you join me in the practice of saying "OK, God" many times each day. That short sentence reflects back to God a willingness to be directed by the Spirit, a submission to him as the Master of the universe, and a trust that he knows what is best for us and for those whose lives we touch.

I invite you to join me in the practice of saying "OK, God" many times each day.

For God did not give us a spirit of timidity, but a spirit of power, of love and of self-discipline. (II Timothy 1:7)

We are told that David was a man after God's own heart. He was the kind of man God approved of and used. He was not perfect, but he did seem to know what was required if he was to be used effectively by God in this world. And the characteristics we have discussed in this chapter are the very things David said had to be true in his life before he was ready to teach.

Let's Review and Evaluate

Are we pure?

Do we keep short accounts with God, making sure we confess every sin that is brought to our minds during our time of examination?

Are we committed?

Are we willing to keep going even when we feel like quitting?

Are we practicing the presence of the Holy Spirit, seeking his guidance and his power for our teaching?

Are we joyful?

Does our joy overflow into our teaching and our relationships with others?

Do we have willingness to do, to be, so say whatever God directs?

If we sense a weakness in any of these areas, the antidote is to talk to God about our concerns. If he has called us to teach, he is eager and willing to make sure we are spiritually prepared to do so. We just need to ask him. Then we say, "OK, God" to whatever he says.

Spiritual preparation is the most important part of the leadership role that God has given us as teachers. God shows us that many times in the Bible. Moses spent eighty years in preparation for the forty years he would lead the people of Israel. After Paul's conversion, he spent three years in separation in Arabia and Damascus before he joined up with the followers of Christ in Jerusalem. The great prophet Elisha spent years under the tutelage of Elijah before he began his ministry. In many ways, we are always in school, always learning, always preparing, always being prepared. The preparation and the power go together.

The next chapters get more into the nitty-gritty of the teaching process and practical suggestions that will help to make us more proficient teachers. But, since we are not dealing with simply learning a skill that can be taught in any secular university, but instead are dealing with teaching the very words of God, I believe it was of vital importance to devote these first two chapters to God's direction of our ministries. Without him, we have nothing to say!

THREE

PREPARING THE MESSAGE

The most precious thing of all is the possibility of being, through the words in my mind or through my inborn unconscious faculties, the recipient of thoughts that come from God.

—Paul Tournier in *The Listening Ear*

You will find these practical pointers as you read this chapter:

- Choosing topics that fit your audience.
- Finding key points to present with emphasis.
- Organizing your message to communicate with clarity.
- Using easy techniques to help students remember your key points.
- Ending your message with a motivational punch.

If you are reading this chapter, I assume you have determined by now that you are called by God to teach his Word and that you are spiritually prepared to do so. The next step is to find out what God wants you to teach. It is pretty exciting to think that he has entrusted us with a message empowered by the Holy Spirit to change the lives of those who hear it. This chapter will outline a plan for getting ready to share that message.

Aiming at Your Audience

When I applied for my first job teaching high school, the principal interviewing me asked, "What do you teach?"

"English," I replied confidently. And, then, lest he not understand the breadth of my ability, I expounded, "Literature, grammar, writing, and speaking."

"Oh," he said quietly, "I was really hoping I would hear you say that you teach kids. I have a lot of people who can teach subject matter, but there are only a few who really understand that teaching means connecting with kids."

I knew instantly that he was right, and it was a lesson I never forgot. I did get the job and enjoyed teaching under the direction of a man who knew the first rule in effective communication: Know your audience and direct your teaching to who they are.

If we are invited to be guest speakers at conferences or retreats, it is wise to ask questions about the people who will attend, about their level of theological understanding, and about the topics and style that they are accustomed to. That does not mean we will not challenge them to step out of their comfort zones, but it means that we will know in advance something about those who will be looking to us for guidance. If there is a gap between their expectations and our delivery, our teaching will not be effective unless we devise ways to bridge that gap.

If we are teachers of an ongoing class, we have an opportunity to know our students more personally. The Saturday morning women's Bible study group I mentioned earlier has met faithfully for five years now. I make it a practice to meet with the women one-on-one whenever possible. Also, as a group, we have held a number of get-togethers just to be able to talk casually and know one another better. Each time we have such an activity and each time I share a cup of coffee or lunch with a woman alone, I learn more about who I am teaching. As I learn what drives them to action and what keeps them awake at night, I am more able to teach to their hearts and not just to their heads.

Have you noticed in the Gospels how Jesus changed his teaching style to suit the position and personality of those he was teaching? He had an advantage that we don't have because he could actually read the thoughts of those he taught. On the other hand, maybe I really don't *want* to know what my students are thinking most of the time! Jesus, though, had that capacity and often addressed the thoughts of his questioners instead of answering their spoken questions directly. He also looked on the crowds and had compassion for them because he saw that they were "harassed and helpless like sheep without a shepherd" (Matthew 9:36). He not only knew their needs, but he empathized with the pain in their lives. His teaching was focused on what they most needed to hear. His example is ours to follow. As we read through the epistles, we realize that Paul, too, knew who he was writing to and was familiar with the idiosyncrasies of the Christians in each city he addressed. You will see a distinct difference in style between what he wrote to the church at Philippi and what he wrote to the churches in Galatia. He knew his audience.

Teachers love to study. I find that a great day for me is one in which I can be at my desk for hours digging into the Bible and commentaries and carefully crafting a killer lesson. But, to be a really good teacher, I have to get out of my study and into the lives of those I teach. That's the only way I can close the gap between the pulpit and the pupil.

Choosing the Topic

It's too bad, but it seems that only rarely can I use a lesson or a message more than once. Because every audience is unique, because every situation has its own nuances and history, and because I keep growing and learning myself, it seems that I am constantly digging into new topics and preparing new materials to teach. The teacher's life would be so easy if that were not the case!

Whether our assignment is a one-time-only message to a Sunday evening Bible study group or an ongoing series of lessons on a topic of our choice, we must choose carefully what we will teach. This is where I like to spend some time in prayerful consideration of various subjects or passages of Scripture and thus allow God to guide my teaching. Most of the time, it seems that the Spirit wants me to teach others what he has been teaching me in my own spiritual journey. The beauty of that plan is that the teaching is then fresh, is out of my personal experience, and is something that helps not only my students but me as well. But I always want my message to be God's message, so I do not proceed with study and lesson planning until I have his clear direction.

Often teachers develop an area of expertise or find that a general theme tends to follow through whatever their topics may be. Ravi Zacharias of Ravi Zacharias International Ministries is a Christian apologist, so often his teaching will relate to the truth of the teachings of Scripture and how those truths relate to human life. Steve Brown of Key Life Ministries states that he has only one topic and it is grace. He teaches through entire books of the Bible, but whatever the passage is that he teaches from, he finds grace and teaches grace to his audiences. Erwin Lutzer of Moody Church says, "This (choosing a topic) is a matter of personal desire combined with what the people need." He goes on to say, "I have been preaching at Moody Church for twenty-five years and have more subjects and ideas in mind than I have time to preach or teach." Warren Wiersbe, who has taught the Bible for more than fifty years, says that, if he is not assigned a topic, he uses the "pray and ponder" method to "see what the Lord is saying to me."

Other master teachers have made the following comments on how they choose topics for teaching:

It is my practice to teach through entire books of the Bible. I often alternate between Old Testament and New Testament books. I usually choose a book based on what I feel the congregation needs at the time. Presently I am teaching through the book of I Peter using the theme of "Hope for Hard Times" as the book of Peter deals a lot with the suffering Christians were undergoing in the early church. I taught a series recently on the life of David during which we looked at a godly life where there was failure and recovery. Sometimes I will break up a long book into several series. For example, when I taught Genesis, I taught on the Life of Abraham, the Life of Joseph, and on the main themes of the entire book.

—Dr. Don Denyes

For preaching, it always a delicate issue to decide on what you perceive the church at large needs and when you do, you preach on it. However, for the most part, I would generally preach expositionally from a book in the Bible. One of the great advantages of this is that you are forced to talk about things you might not usually choose to talk about.

—Rev. William Dondit

Choosing a topic is a matter of personal desire combined with what the people need. I like doing topics of interest. I think we should teach about the controlling realities of our culture such as same sex marriage, *The DaVinci Code*, and most of all, those truths from the Bible that will bring transformation of life and heart.

—Dr. Erwin Lutzer

I like to teach on cutting edge topics such as abortion, just war, gambling, and so on … Application is important. I often ask pastors, "What do you read?" We must relate our material to what our audience is thinking about or living. We need to help people do moral reasoning on issues. We get Christian kids from Christian homes who can quote Bible verses but cannot tell the relevance of a Bible story to today. Christ taught so people could "get it".

—Dr. Rex Rogers

I struggle with the question of choice of topics now more than at any other time in my ministry. First, I pray. Then I try to sense the need within the church. I seek input from others concerning that need as well. I think about the balance of material (e.g. If I have been teaching entirely from the New Testament for some time, I may choose an Old Testament series to provide balance). Then I wait until something catches fire.

—Dr. Bill Rudd

My approach has been two-fold. One, to take the Scriptures and preach from those passages that address the searching questions of the audience. The context of one's preaching must deal with felt issues. This is even more important for the itinerant because he or she does not have the luxury of systematic weekly teaching.

—Dr. Ravi Zacharias

In my own teaching, I find that I emphasize themes of simplifying our lives so that we can focus on God and relationship with him. Much of my teaching has to do with the practice of spiritual disciplines to develop of our awareness of the eternal world. To be sure, I teach about truth and grace, too, but my passion is for helping others develop a personal, intimate relationship with God; so I find myself returning over and over again to that theme.

Teachers do not have to specialize, but sometimes it just happens. If you are not sure of what your overarching theme might be, think for a moment of what God is teaching you. Then review some of the topics you have chosen to teach over the past few years and just see if there is a pattern that emerges. If not, just keep following your heart and God's. Your students will be the beneficiaries of the topics you choose.

Another matter to consider as we develop our gifts is the teaching method we use for any given study. Some teachers are consistent in teaching through an entire book of the Bible in order not to miss a message that God has intended for us. Others use topical studies so that what they teach will be specifically relevant in the lives of their students. I believe that both methods are in keeping with biblical principles, so use whichever method you are comfortable with for a given group and time.

I tend to alternate between verse-by-verse studies of books of the Bible and thematic studies. Sometimes I can combine the two. I recently finished teaching a series entitled "Look What Grace Can Do!" Essentially it was a study of the book of Hebrews. We went verse by verse through the book, but our goal was to see the grace of God at work as we studied the text. Another time I taught through the book of Joshua chapter by chapter, but then added a concluding lesson entitled "Joshua's Rock Group," which reviewed all the ways in which stones were important in the life of Joshua. The title intrigued my students; and, by teaching this way, I was able to combine the historical study— which, of course, had its own applications each week—with a more symbolic, thematic study that examined some key points in Joshua's life and helped all of us to understand better the importance of looking back to see where God has been at work in our lives.

Reviewing the Materials

When I have chosen or been assigned a topic for teaching, I begin to gather all the information I have on the topic: books, Internet resources, and articles I have clipped. A later chapter will address the various resources available and filing systems for gathering our own materials, but for now we will assume that we have access to the materials we need. As I prepare, I read in gulps, gathering concepts and drinking in viewpoints of other experts on the subject. When I encounter ideas I believe are relevant to the group I am about to teach—or to me personally—I make some notes, keeping in mind that if I use an idea, approach, or turn of phrase from another Bible teacher or author, I must give credit to its originator. It's OK to learn from one another, but we, as Christian teachers, must never claim

It's OK to learn from one another, but we, as Christian teachers, must never claim as ours a thought that we gleaned from another believer.

as ours a thought that we gleaned from another believer. Our students won't care that the idea did not originate with us; the main point is that, by all means available to us, we honestly and passionately deliver the truth on our hearts. But we must never dishonor the name of God by taking credit for something that is not originally ours.

Once I have read as much as I can readily find and absorb by other authors on the topic, I move to the biblical text. Using a concordance, I check all the relevant passages of Scripture that might help me to teach what the Bible says specifically concerning the subject matter at hand. Now, I am reading more slowly, contemplating what I read, and asking for the Holy Spirit's guidance in what he wants me to learn and—knowing that—what he wants me to teach. My notes at this point are more detailed and more specifically related to Scripture.

At times we may begin with the biblical text and then consult other resources. At other times we are compelled by a topic or theme and may begin with what others have written. The order of the reading is not necessarily important. The point is that we need to read both the Bible to see what God has to say about the subject and other authors and scholars to benefit from their knowledge and application. Once we have reviewed information from these sources, we are ready to zero in on the specific message that we will present.

Gleaning Main Points

At this point in my preparation, I go back over the notes I have taken and, almost without fail, a pattern emerges. This is where, for me, the getting ready process really starts to be exhilarating and fun. I begin to see the really important things that I need to teach about the subject matter. I begin to sense the leading of the Spirit in discerning the needs of my audience and the benefits they might receive from the teaching that is unfolding in front of me.

Often, at this step in the process, I approach a difficult crossroads. I usually have a number of points that seem important, and I have the difficult task of choosing those that are the most significant for this group at this time. As teachers, we take in a lot more than we can teach in any given lesson. We must discipline ourselves to sort through to the real core of the message remembering that

- to our students, this material will be new. We have had a chance to chew on it for awhile, but they haven't.
- they will be taking it in aurally and not reading and processing as we have done.
- they have limited attention spans and can absorb only what we can give them in a short period of time.
- they will be listening, but their minds will also be wandering (try not to be offended, but even the best speakers cannot keep the full mental attention of their audiences all the time).
- they will walk away remembering one or two main points, but no more.

So, keeping those restrictions in mind, we must limit the points we teach and then bolster each point with illustrations, discussion, and repetition so that they will truly be memorable after the class walks out the door.

Once I have my main points firmly established, I challenge myself to write one succinct sentence defining the primary goal in the teaching of this lesson. If my class is going to remember only one thing from what they hear me say, what do I want it to be? That sentence forms a focal point that I envision as I begin to flesh out the methods and means I'll use to present the message. Everything from this point on in my preparation and presentation will work toward keeping the message of truth firmly directed toward that focal point. If I have an illustration or a point that does not contribute to that primary point, I discard it, even if it's really good. The discipline of defining my specific goal helps me to focus the teaching so that it is clear to me—and only then will it be clear to those who are learning from me.

Formulating an Outline

Here's where we can get creative. If you love words as much as I do, you will have a great time trying to put together an outline that helps your students remember what you are teaching. Here are a few techniques that might be helpful:

- Alliteration. Memory is aided if the primary words of each main point begin with the same letter. I taught a series on the Book of Judges once and when we came to Ehud, the lefthanded judge, the outline I used was this:

Creativity
Courage
Collaboration

My goal was that, by the end of the lesson the students would remember that they were each endowed with unique attributes that God wants them to put to use *creatively*, that they may need to be *courageous* in putting those abilities to work, and they would be most effective if they *collaborated* with other Christians. Alliteration helped them remember these points.

- Parallel structure. Another way to help students remember our main points is to write them in a pattern so that the first one will give a clue to the second, and so on. When I taught a series on the Ten Commandments, the outline for the command against murder looked like this:

Understanding the command
Violating the command
Recognizing murder
Embracing life

Each point in the outline was a verb-object pattern. One thought led into the other so that the lesson began with a negative instruction and ended with a positive challenge. The lesson on the commandment against stealing used an outline that consisted of four nouns that illuminated our relationship to material possessions:

Ownership
Honesty
Contentment
Generosity

The thought flowed from what we own through to having a heart that is willing to share.

- Acronym/acrostic. As I write this, I am also preparing to teach three sessions at a women's retreat for a church in our area. A spa theme has been chosen by the retreat committee as they are encouraging women to get away for a time of relaxation and refreshment. I have selected the themes of my three teaching sessions accordingly and have entitled them as follows:

  Simplify (stripping away all that is not important so that we can focus on our relationship with God)
  Purify (keeping short accounts with God; getting cleaned up so that we can be useful in serving him)
  Attach (relating to other people, particularly family and fellow Christians)

My hope is that when the women go home from their spa weekend, the word *spa* will help them to remember the lessons they have been taught.

One word of caution: If you want your acronym to be remembered, keep it short. I remember a youth retreat I attended where the speaker used the acronym WATERMELON. We didn't think he would ever get done, and I certainly couldn't tell you a week later what each of those letters stood for!

- Repetition. Sometimes repeating a key word throughout each main point will help your listeners to recall all the points you are making. One of the most memorable speeches given by Winston Churchill was to a graduating class at Harrow School in 1941. You may remember these words: "Never give in— never, never, never, never, in nothing great or small, great or petty, never give in except to convictions of honour or good sense. Never yield to force; never yield to the apparently overwhelming might of the enemy" (www.quotationspage. com).

The skillful use of repetition embedded into the minds of the graduates the importance of persistence even in the face of the grave dangers of World War II.

In one lesson I presented to a Bible study group, I emphasized the importance of total commitment to God. I used the following repetitive outline:

> Radical perspectives
> Radical relationships
> Radical rewards

Even if the class did not remember the details of the lesson, I hope that they remembered that God wants us to be radical for him!

- Word picture. Creating a visual image in the minds of your students will help them to recall your teaching. A great example of this is the armor of God that Paul describes in Ephesians 6. When we read this passage, we can visualize the soldier (or, in Paul's case, probably the guard at his door) with the helmet of salvation on his head and the sword of the Spirit in his hand.

Packing a Punch

At this point in our planning, we go back to the theme sentence that we talked about earlier. Before we can bring our presentation to a successful conclusion, we remind ourselves where we intended to go and honestly assess: Did we get there? We review the outline we have assembled and make sure that everything in that outline points toward the focal point. Eliminate anything that might be a distraction to that goal, keeping in mind that our students can only hold one or two main points in their heads as they listen to us. That is not a criticism of our students nor of the quality of our teaching, but a simple fact of pedagogy: if we throw out too much information, it will not be

Our students are listening, not reading. They are hearing, not seeing. Therefore, we must keep our message tightly focused from beginning to end.

retained. Our students are listening, not reading. They are hearing, not seeing. Therefore, we must keep our message tightly focused from beginning to end.

Knowing that focus helps us know how to conclude our lesson. As someone once said, in a good speech you tell your audience what you are going to say, you say it, and then you tell them what you said. A good lesson is the same. We give the students our focus at the beginning, and then everything we say works to support our reaching that goal. At the conclusion of our lesson, we have our final opportunity to guide their minds and hearts to the core of our message. When we do, our students will have learned and, by God's grace, lives will be changed.

There are several ways to end our lessons with that kind of impact.

- Reminder. Somewhere near the end of the lesson, we must remind our students what the focal point was. We told them at the beginning where we were heading, and we have provided supporting material along the way. We now need to remind them of the main point. It should have greater impact now than it did when we first presented it because now we have guided them to the validity of the point and helped them understand its importance in their lives.

- Story. There is probably no better place for a story that has emotional impact than at the end of the message. Our students have been following our teaching of facts, points, and scriptural understandings. Now we can bring it home by telling a story that touches their hearts. By making emotional contact after laying the intellectual groundwork, we are positioning our students to leave our classroom ready for action. Their motivation to change or act will arise from our ability to reach them at their emotional cores. Nothing will do that more effectively than a well chosen story or illustration. There are many sources for these stories, but I have found that the most effective are those that come from my own life. Students relate to teachers who are willing to show their own vulnerability by sharing relevant life experiences.

- Quote. There are people who have a gift of saying something in a way that is memorable and full of impact. I can think of no more powerful way to conclude a teaching on commitment to God than with D. L. Moody's quote, "The world has yet to see what God can do with a man who is fully committed to Him." It's short, it's memorable, it's challenging; and it was spoken by someone who exhibited an admirable commitment to God, yet knew there could be more.

We want to make it easy for our students to remember the focal point of our message. If you find a quote that does that, use it. It will be powerful if used at the end of the presentation because it will be one of the last things your students hear before they leave your lesson that day. If you want to make sure they remember it, repeat it two or three times. If it is good, it will bear repeating; and very seldom do any of us remember a quote we hear only once. If it is more than a couple of lines long, you may want to include it printed in full in the outline that you will pass out to students when they come in. We will talk in more detail about that outline in the next chapter.

- Summary. A tried-and-true method of ending a lesson is to summarize the main points of your presentation. Again, repetition aids memory. If our outlines are alliterated, logical, sequential; if they feature points with first letters forming acronyms or being parallel in structure; they will be remembered more easily. If we remind our students of our goal, summarize the points that have been made along the way, and then tie in the goal once again, they have a better chance of walking away with a true grasp of the points of the lesson.

- Questions. There are times when we want our students to ponder ideas we have presented. Maybe we have challenged them to think or to relate more fully to God or to each other. Maybe we have raised issues for which there are no pat answers. With these kinds of topics, an effective close to the lesson might be a short series of questions that will enable them to zero in on the points presented. Maybe we have talked about the importance of living a life of purity. We have given biblical examples and supportive scriptural passages. We have provided illustrations of one or two individuals who answered God's call to purity and whose lives were changed as a result. We now want to bring the message to its intrinsic goal: changed lives in those who are hearing our teaching. We might close with questions like these:

What areas of your life would not pass the scriptural purity test?

Are you willing to give up specific activities or relationships you are involved in that displease your heavenly Father?

Would you commit to spending some time alone with God in the next twenty-four hours to allow the Holy Spirit to work a work of grace in your life so that you can present your body as a living sacrifice, holy and acceptable to God?

- Challenge. Sometimes we want to make sure our listeners go away with something specific to do. When that is the case, a conclusion that calls for action is appropriate. We must make the instructions as specific, as clear, and as memorable as possible. I heard a sermon by Bill Hybels, senior pastor of Willow Creek Church just outside of Chicago, in which he quoted a sermon by an African-American preacher whose church he happened to visit while on vacation. The preacher had talked about the Good Samaritan and ended with Jesus's directive to the expert in the law, "Go and do likewise." Jesus gave a specific, clear, and powerful call to action. However, the African-American preacher wanted to take that call and apply it effectively to his congregation, so he summarized it as "Go and do." Then he said those words over and over again until the entire congregation was saying rhythmically with him, "Go and do. Go and do. Go and do. Go and do!" If they didn't hear any other points in that sermon, they knew that they needed to go out and do good to others around them. After hearing Hybels recount the lesson, I, too, began to remind myself to "Go and do." It was a powerful call to action!

 ## Let's Review and Evaluate

Are we taking time to take a good look at our material and find the key points that we need to teach?

Are we organizing our thoughts in such a way that they are clearly communicable to our students?

Are we creatively thinking of ways to make our points memorable so that our students will walk out of our class mulling over what was presented in our message?

Are we bold enough to end our lesson with a challenge so that the teaching that is given will take hold and result in changed lives?

If we are consistently doing these things, we are providing a vehicle through which the Word of God can work with effectiveness—first in us and then in our students.

FOUR

PRESENTING THE MESSAGE

He mobilized the English language and sent it into battle.

—John F. Kennedy
referring to the speeches of Winston Churchill during World War II

This chapter will give these practical guides for making a powerful presentation:

- Getting the audience to like you.
- Making sure your voice and words are pleasant and easy to understand.
- Helping your listeners follow your train of thought.
- Connecting with the emotions of your students.
- Inspiring your audience to action.

I remember one of the first public speaking engagements I had. I was really excited about the invitation to give a message to a group of about fifty women. I prepared and prepared and *prepared* my talk on the book of Ruth. I knew more about Ruth than I thought there was to know. And I was eager to share all my freshly gained knowledge with the women who, I was sure, were eagerly awaiting my words of wisdom.

The evening came and I began to have second thoughts. Why did I agree to do this? I have limited experience as a speaker. They are probably expecting someone much more polished than I was. How could I hold their attention for the whole forty minutes? I was pretty nervous by the time the group leader introduced me.

After I got up to the platform and adjusted and re-adjusted my lapel microphone (It was the first time I had used one!), I began to talk. The more I talked, the more I liked to talk. I looked at the ladies in the audience. They were listening! Whew! I did have too many points and too much to tell them in the time allotted, but I managed to get through the core points of the message, turned the podium over to the leader for the closing, and sat down wondering what had just happened. I had moved into my "zone." The time flew and I was having fun! The sheer exhilaration of completing the daunting task and receiving positive feedback afterward made all the doubts and anxieties fade into oblivion.

That's what teaching has become for me: moments of joy, followed by moments of sheer terror, followed by the flow of the message, followed by a sense of accomplishment and, sometimes, even exhilaration. Who wants life to be just flat? The ups and downs of teaching and speaking keep me fully alive. Maybe you have experienced something similar.

As I have developed speaking skills, I have discovered that there are a few helpful guidelines that we all can benefit from as we deliver our messages. In this chapter, we will present some of those tips and, in that way, will help us all to continue to improve the art of presentation so that our teaching will be well received and easily assimilated into the lives of our students.

Gentle on the Eyes

As Christians, and even more so as teachers of other Christians, we are representatives of God on earth. Our goal should be not to have people look *at* us, but look *through* us to see our Father in Heaven. It is as if we are panes of glass. The cleaner the glass, the more clearly will be the vision of God that is seen through us. If we smear up that glass with distracting impressions, the view of God will not be as clear. Instead, the smudges will call attention to the pane of glass and will block the view of the holy God that we want our students to enjoy. How do we make sure that their spiritual eyes are not on us, but on God himself?

We may not like it, but the fact is that people do tend to judge us by the way we look. In order to be effective teachers of the Bible, we do not necessarily have to be beautiful or handsome, but we do need to present ourselves well to those who are looking to us as examples of what God can do in the life of his followers.

- First impression. Someone once said, "You have only one chance to make a first impression." As you walk across the stage to the lectern, your students are already forming an opinion of you. Is your walk firm and confident? Do you stand straight and move with energy? Do you have a friendly expression on your face? Would those watching you think you are glad to be there? Or would they see you as hesitant, anxious, or wishing this whole ordeal were over?

  We might also keep in mind that even before we get behind the lectern, we are being observed. As you visit with people before giving your message, know you are being evaluated. Talk to a few people as you come into the room. There is a side benefit to this cordiality: When you get up to speak, you will be surprised at how good it feels to fix your eyes on some friendly faces in the audience because at least some of the people you greeted will feel like they know you already.

- Outward appearance. It does matter what you look like. If you are going to stand in front of a group for thirty to sixty minutes, care enough to look your best. Dress appropriately. Make sure you have clothing that allows you to move your arms freely. Women, make sure that you are dressed modestly. You don't have to be a prude, and you should be up-to-date in styles, but skirt lengths should be at or below the knee and blouse necklines should not be revealing. Men, make sure that your clothing is pressed, brushed, and spotless and your shoes are polished.

  For me, the rule of thumb is that the speaker should always be dressed just one notch more formally than the audience. When my Saturday morning Bible study meets, most of the women wear jeans. I usually choose to wear sport and dress slacks and never wear jeans when I teach. If I am teaching at an evening function where the attendees will be wearing dress slacks, I will wear a suit, either with slacks or a skirt. As teachers of God's Word, we need to project authority and command respect, and dressing the part helps to encourage that.

- Physical condition. One of my pet peeves is watching a televised Christian broadcast featuring a preacher or teacher who has allowed his or her appearance to become untended or unattractively presented. I am sure I will get e-mails about how wrong it is for me to judge, but if I, a committed Christian, am distracted from the message by the seeming lack of self control or attention to appearance of the messenger, wouldn't non-Christians be even more put off by the same thing? If we are going to be in the public eye, and if we are setting ourselves up as examples to those who learn from us, it is our responsibility to take good care of our bodies. We do not have to fit the model image that Hollywood projects (nearly *all* of us would have to quit if that were the case!), but we do need to be comfortable with the way we look and show the outside world that we value the bodies God has given us.

Another element is physical fitness. Your voice will be clearer, your capacity to stand and move better, and your appearance more appealing if you exercise regularly. My personal regimen includes a variety of exercise, but for at least a short time every day, I am focused on disciplining my body so that I can be in as good health as possible to be available to do God's work wherever and whenever he might send me. A good soldier has to be conditioned and ready to go! Please don't misunderstand: You do not have to be thin, tan, and toned in order to be used by God. But I do believe it is our responsibility, given the physical bodies we have been given, to present ourselves in the best possible way so that our message can be heard and will not be discredited by our appearance.

Pleasant to the Ear

When we are presenting a message we believe in, our audience will be less distracted and more tuned in if we deliver it in a way that promotes good listening. This involves both what we say and how we say it.

- Opening words. Just as the first visual impression that our audiences gets of us is important, so is the first sentence that we say when we get to the lectern. Whether it is a class we teach every week or a one-time speaking engagement, within the first few seconds our students will decide whether or not we have something worth saying. So we strive to deliver an opening line or two that wins them to us. One thing every audience likes to hear is that we are glad to be there. Seems trite, I know, but it's true. Those listening want to know that we like them, that we are sincerely honored to have been asked to be there, and that we are looking out for their best interest. Once we win their allegiance, they are more likely to want to listen to our message. Another way to win over an audience is with humor. An opening anecdote or a slightly self-deprecating remark will get them laughing and engender a camaraderie that will prepare our students to listen to us with open and friendly ears.

  After the initial greetings and comments, we should launch immediately into our topic. No matter if it is a new group or one that I know intimately, I try to begin with something that gets the gray matter moving. Maybe a question will do it. Or a story. Or a succinct quote. Or an accounting of something I saw on the news that relates to the theme of my teaching. Because my students are coming from busy, distracting lives, I realize that the first thing I have to do is capture their attention away from those distractions and to the topic at hand.

- Confidence. As a presenter, you are considered an expert, whether you feel that you are or not. The better you know your subject matter, the less you have to rely on your notes; and the more confidently you speak, the more likely you will be to keep the attention of your audience. There are two very important points to remember here: 1. Know your material well and practice it until you can present it with a certain boldness, and 2. Once you have done your homework, rely on the Holy Spirit to be your guide and teacher in recalling the right points to emphasize and in presenting the message in a way that honors the God you serve.

• Voice. Have you heard your voice? Really heard it? If you want to improve your presentation voice, get or borrow a really good voice recorder and listen to what others hear. Or, if you are making a public presentation, ask the host to record your speech. You will find it extremely helpful to listen to the way you sound when you are actually in front of a group.

A few years ago a research group surveyed people to determine what kinds of voices were most irritating. Nearly half of the respondents most disliked the nasal sound, which they described as a whiny, complaining voice. Others that were not well received included high-pitched, loud, and monotonous voices *(How to Say It with Your Voice*, p. 61).

If you listen to your recorded voice, you can judge for yourself whether your vocal quality can be improved. Being conscious of the need for change is the first step. One of the best exercises I have found is to read aloud. You might try it, too. Listen to yourself as you read short passages. Consciously change the quality of your voice to reduce nasal tones, to soften sharpness, and to project clearly. Or, recite simple poems, Bible verses, or song lyrics as you drive in your car. Practice makes perfect, even when we are changing something as basic as the way we sound. We don't all have radio announcer voices, but we all can learn to train our voices so that we can be heard and so that the sound that comes out of our mouths will be listenable.

• Speech habits. Identifying annoying speech habits is another thing we can learn by listening to a recording of ourselves. Is our speech peppered with long pauses? Or with "uhs," "ands," or "ahs" as we search for the next word? Do we sound unnatural or affected? Do we click our tongues or swallow noticeably? Some of these mannerisms are response to the stress of being center stage and are probably not noticed by us as speakers. Again, awareness is half the battle. A voice or video recording will help you find and eliminate the mannerisms that detract from your message.

- Modulation. There is nothing that will put a class to sleep faster than a monotone. We may have the most exciting lesson in the world to present, but if our delivery is flat, we won't convince or convict our audience. So, we have to practice putting variety into our voices: volume, tone, level of emphasis. Most speech coaches advise that we do not have to fear over-dramatizing. A little extra emphasis may seem theatrical to us, but it will most likely convey sincerity and interest to our listeners. The end result will be that our message will be more believable because our audience will sense our conviction of its importance and of its relevance to their lives.

- Enunciation. Have you ever received a voice-mail message with words so run together that you can scarcely figure out what the caller is trying to convey? It is frustrating to decipher the message and, you might conclude, the caller didn't think the message very important to you or he or she might certainly have slowed down enough to enunciate clearly. The most common enunciation problem is the slurring or dropping of the final consonant sounds in words. We can overcome these lazy patterns by reading out loud and exaggerating our pronunciation to make sure we are enunciating all the necessary sounds in each word and especially concluding consonants. Clear enunciation means our students do not have to be frustrated by *almost* understanding what we are trying to say. If they have to listen too hard, they will stop listening sooner.

- Pace. This is one of my biggest problems. After I have studied hard to prepare a good lesson, I have a lot I want to say and, erroneously, I think that if I say it faster, I will communicate more. Also, the nervous energy that goes into presenting a message revs up my engine so that I am tempted to talk at a pace that makes my words less comprehensible. Most speakers need to slow down. Because I had an awareness that this was a problem for me, at one presentation where I had a good friend in the audience, I asked her to give me a signal if she thought I needed to slow my rate of delivery. She didn't have to give me the high sign, after all, because every time I looked at her, I remembered that she was monitoring my pace, and that caused me to do the same. As with all of our presentation issues, self awareness is of primary importance.

You may have noted a recurring theme in this section, and that is the importance of recording and listening to ourselves. I cannot emphasize this enough. Hearing our voices, inflections, and vocal mannerisms is enlightening and gives us information we cannot access in any other way. My husband is a musician and he, too, is on the "record and listen" bandwagon. He will tape a practice piece, critique it as he listens to the recording, and then practice areas that need improvement. After his practice time, he records the piece again to see if he did, in fact, do a better job on the weak areas. If your discipline has to do with making sounds, recording and listening is an important tool in improving those sounds.

Accessible to the Mind

As I mentioned earlier, we are presenting points and truths that we have spent many hours preparing. In our delivery, though, we have to remember that this material is new to our audience and, therefore, it is imperative that we make a focused effort to help them understand and remember our points. Here are a few ways to do that with effectiveness.

- Main points. Keep your main points few and make them memorable. In Chapter 3, I described how to formulate an outline with parallel structure, alliteration, or similar technique to help our listeners remember what we are teaching. Three main points are usually about all that students can absorb and remember if they are simply sitting through a speech. If it is a study session where they have outlines in front of them and are taking notes, we can present more points. Even then, though, we must remember that our goal is changed lives. If our students walk away muddled or overstimulated with new ideas, their intellects will be tickled, but their lives may not be changed. Sincerely presenting just one, two, or three main points gives us a better chance of penetrating the heart and the will.

- Repetition. In earlier times, when someone heard a speech, they heard it once. There were no recordings, instant replays, or videotapes to enable them to review what the speaker had said. Speakers in that day were well aware that, if their hearers did not remember the first time, the message would be lost forever. So good presenters developed the art of repetition. Even today, speech coaches (as I have already mentioned, but this *is* the section on repetition!) will tell us to open our message by telling the audience what we are going to say, then telling them what we want to say, and concluding by reminding them what we have said. At each of these junctures, we are reminding our students of the roadmap we are following throughout the speech. That roadmap helps them to follow our path of thought and, if we are effective, will also enable them to reach the same conclusions we have reached and which we are now trying so sincerely to communicate.

If we're communicating a key principle, repeating it multiple times throughout our presentation will embed it in the minds of our hearers. Repetition of a key phrase is also a great memory aid. One of the most famous from history is Abraham Lincoln's Gettysburg Address in which he said, in part, "That government *of the people, by the people, for the people*, shall not perish from the earth." (Italics added.) His emphasis? People. That message is clearly communicated in a fashion that has been remembered for nearly one and a half centuries now. Don't we all wish that the truths we convey will be so well preserved!

- Memory aids. The current term for the use of visual, aural, and mnemonic aids is *mediating*. It means using various media to transmit our message. I like that term because it reminds me of what Jesus did. He became the mediator between us and God. He was the ultimate visual aid! It takes a great deal of effort to find just the right video clip, recording, work of art, or newspaper article to illustrate our point, but when we are dealing with today's audiences, who are accustomed to being bombarded with visual images and sounds, we may have to get into their heads and hearts by using media. The general rule is that the more of the five senses we can stimulate, the more memorable our message will be. Cornerstone College President Rex Rogers reiterates this point, "I find that I am mediating more of what I do. I use video clips, pictures, and multilevel presentations in order to involve more of the senses of my students or listeners. That's the direction of our culture today."

Understood by the Heart

As teachers of the Bible, our goal is changed lives, not the simple communication of facts. In order to approach transformation, we must access the emotions of our listeners. There are a few ways that help us do that.

- Stories/illustrations. I am convinced that the best teachers are the best story tellers. Why are stories so important? Because they touch the heart. Delivery of a lesson or a sermon or a message without touching the hearts of the listeners is equivalent to the resounding gong and clanging cymbal of I Corinthians 13. One of the best ways to have emotional impact on our students is through stories. There are many resources through which we can find stories to bring our points home: books, Internet, newspapers, novels, and our own experience. Even those unwanted forwarded e-mails sometimes yield great

  One of the best ways to have emotional impact on our students is through stories.

stories. Richard Dowis in *The Lost Art of the Great Speech* gives the following criteria for an effective story or impactful illustration for a message:

It must be true, or at least perceived to be true.

It must give insight into the nature of the subject, the speaker, or the event.

It must be interesting or amusing.

It must be simple enough for the audience to grasp easily.

It must illustrate, support, or lead to a point that the speaker has made or wants to make. (p. 159)

Once you find a story that meets these criteria, practice telling it so that your listener is led along with you to the life-changing point you want to deliver. I heard an author being interviewed on the radio recently, and she said that we remember a certain percentage of what we hear, a greater percentage of what we hear *and* see, but 100 percent of what we *feel*. Stories that are chosen carefully and told effectively can connect with our students' feelings and, thus, will help them commit our message to memory and to practice.

- Concluding challenge. Because we are teachers who want to effect change in the lives of our students, we should never let them walk out the door without a specific challenge. What do we want them to do or be as a result of the lesson we teach? Do we want them to be more loving? More generous? More forgiving? More responsible? More prayerful? More disciplined? We need to pick the one (and *only* one) target that was our goal as we prepared our message, then reiterate that goal as a concluding guideline. Maybe we will need to summarize our main points first, but our final words should be a resounding statement or picture of what they should desire to become as they put into practice what we have taught.

How the Experts Do It

My friend Phyllis Nye, who taught speech for thirty-plus years, has a way of making things easy for us. She says that there are really only three basic rules for making an effective presentation: Have something to say, say what you mean, and care if they listen. In her words, "Adherence to these rules will cause you to do a lot of things right without any special training."

Other master teachers provide us with these insights for presenting our message in a style that suits and reaches our students:

My style … is direct, persuasive, passionate, challenging, and calling for decisions. It's rather a no-nonsense approach.

—Rev. William Dondit

I would hope that my teaching style would be creative, interactive, and discussion oriented. I am pretty opposed to the "talking head" approach and don't necessarily feel that it is helpful in teaching. Even when I lead retreats, I find myself asking my audience often for their insights. "What popped off the page to you?" I use a mutual approach to unpackaging Scripture.

—Jo Kadlecek

I am no longer rigid. I always feel that, as a teacher, I am creating a tapestry, weaving together all the threads of curriculum, classroom activities, and other experiences which touch the lives of my students.

—Nataly Berckmann

My style is both informative and transformational, conveying content and application. Someone once told me, "Don't forget the 'so what?'" I have remembered that ever since. I hope my style is more personal and conversational than preachy and rhetorical. I do more expositional teaching than other kinds, but I am not locked into expositional teaching only. I try to be constantly looking at how my style should be varied or changed. Most of the Bible is narrative and I am sensing that I need to use more narrative style and stories in my teaching. There is no single method or style for connecting with a changing culture.

—Dr. Bill Rudd

I am not a lecturer. I like to pose questions and get people thinking. I search for issues and lead discussions with my students, encouraging them to discover truths for themselves. In adult Bible study, this format works very effectively. With college students, more direction may be needed and the activities may need to be broken up in order to keep the attention of the class. It is always important to bring in an application. I challenge them to think and then to discuss how to apply the learning with what they are going through. God speaks through his Word and through other people, too. We enlighten one another.

—Kathleen O. Sindorf

I would say most of my speaking is an "argument style." By that I do not mean argumentative. I mean building one block at a time and taking one step of reason at a time until the truth is evident and the heart exposed to its own arrogance. But the conviction can only come from the Holy Spirit. I jokingly say that I am not skilled in *Power Point.* I lean on the Spirit for the power as I try to make the point. It really is a combination of argument and story that bridges the head to the heart, appealing then to the will.

— Dr. Ravi Zacharias

I am somewhat eclectic in style, depending on the audience, subject matter, time factors, and other variables. But my overall style is to combine a Socratic method of give and take with students, followed by a synthesis of ideas which are shaped around a core set of principles or ideas which I am hoping my students will take away from our time together.

—Dr. Ron Mahurin

A teaching style must be part of who you are. You may adapt others' techniques, but they must be tweaked to fit your personality.

—Phyllis Nye

I feed the lambs and sheep, not the giraffes. I aim at simplicity, because the simple truths are the most profound.

—Dr. Warren Wiersbe

As teachers, we must remember that our presentation is the way we put a frame around our message. Many of us love to study and, thus, we spend hours in preparation of teaching down to the minutest of details, but we sometimes forget that style, comportment, and speech are the contexts in which that message can be effectively delivered. Jesus himself understood that when he said in John 12:49, "For I did not speak of my own accord, but the Father who sent me commanded me *what to say* and *how to say it*." (Emphasis mine). Jesus is the Master Teacher. We would do well to emulate him!

Measuring Your Results

Feedback from students helps us to know if we are really connecting. If we are speaking to a large group, it may be difficult to tell how well we have conveyed the message of our hearts. Eye contact will help, as will actual response—if we ask for evidence of a commitment (show of hands, standing, signing card, asking questions, etc.). Many teachers state that the best way to tell if connection has been made is by the verbal feedback received immediately after the presentation. Are we getting specific comments about what point touched our hearers or are we getting generalized statements about its being a "good message"? Usually we can conclude that the more specific the comments, the more effective the presentation.

Some of the master teachers gave the following insights on assessing our effectiveness:

Often I don't know if I have successfully conveyed my message. The only way I really know is if they tell me. Otherwise, I have just to be faithful to what I am trying to do. When Mother Theresa won the Nobel Peace Prize, a reporter asked her how it felt to be so successful. She answered, "God never called me to be successful. He called me to be faithful." We all are on different journeys. We all learn differently.

—Dr. Tamara Rosier

Measuring the success of a teaching is one of the most difficult things to do. Sometimes, the preacher can come away totally discouraged and yet people see it as a good sermon. Sometimes I can tell if I am connecting by watching faces of my listeners or by the activity or lack thereof in the audience. If I am losing them and can see it, I have an opportunity to adapt or adjust the presentation. The best measure is over the long haul—are lives being changed?

—Dr. Don Denyes

I try not to get caught up in the notion of "successfulness" since so much of teaching is about matters of the heart which are not easily measured.

—Dr. Ron Mahurin

The harvest is not the end of the meeting, but the end of the age. One day, we'll see what the Lord did through us and in spite of us.

—Dr. Warren Wiersbe

I can tell by the look on a few faces when I have made a connection. They just light up! Then I double back and pick up the faces that are not lit until they get it, too. It is a real joy to see students put into action something I have taught.

—Phyllis Nye

When you have succeeded, it is written on the faces of the people and affirmed afterwards, not just by friends but also by those who may not have been sympathetic to your subject in the first place. The key is to make sure you have conveyed truth without compromise, but doing so sensitively so as to get the one with a contrary position to respect your authenticity and your understanding of the subject.

—Dr. Ravi Zacharias

I sometimes see an "aha!" moment in someone's eyes. Or I know I have connected when they begin to talk about things that they have been thinking about. The feedback they give is an indicator of the extent to which they have understood.

—Kathleen O. Sindorf

The feedback we get is not the final arbiter of our effectiveness, but we can use the responses to continue doing what works and to revise what doesn't. As long as we are human beings delivering messages to other human beings, there will be room for improvement!

Let's Review and Evaluate

How are we doing in our presentation?

Do we look our best so that we can point people to God and his Word without their being distracted by our appearance?

Do we seek to meet our listeners at their emotional and spiritual center?

Do we find ways to get our points across that will be memorable and life-changing?

Do we practice until we are so familiar with the material that we cease relying only on our notes and, instead, allow the Spirit to guide as we present our lesson?

FIVE

CONNECTING WITH STUDENTS

By being true I am allowing people to get to know the real me, and it feels better to have people love the real me than the me I invented.

—Don Miller in *Blue Like Jazz*

This chapter will give you some ideas for making sure you are truly connecting with your students. As you read, you will find ways to … :

- Watch for changed thinking in your students.
- Use personal life experiences to relate to your audience.
- Get to know your audience as a group and one-on-one.
- Create effective assignments.
- Ask for honest feedback.

W hen I asked him how he knew that he had connected successfully to those he taught, Michigan pastor Bill Rudd said, "By life changes. In the past, I would have thought that success would have been measured by content retention. Not any more. Content is important, but transformation is more important."

In education, we have moved way beyond the model where the teacher is a source of information that the students must take in and then parrot back. Leonard Sweet calls this the "big jug, little mug" theory of education. The teacher is the big jug of data and knowledge and pours it into the little mugs of the students who then go happily away with full mugs, coming back the next day or the next week for refills. Before the days of the Internet and the availability of vast amounts of information, that model was effective. Now it seems that information is not the issue, application is. And there is no place where the application trumps the information more dramatically than in spiritual teaching.

Teaching is not only about helping our students know what we know. It is infinitely more than that. When we teach successfully, we are helping others to think bigger, more creative, and more profound thoughts; and we are helping them to become more Christ-like in their attitudes, their understanding, and their actions. The sheer magnitude of that assignment probably makes us tremble a little inside. But if we had a goal any less lofty, it would not be worthy of the God we serve.

As I mentioned in the last chapter, it's difficult to know whether we've achieved that goal. How do we measure transformation? How do we know we are making a real difference in the lives of those we teach? Sometimes we don't. Teaching involves a lot of faith. Sometimes we teach just because God told us to do it, we trust that the outcome of our teaching will bring honor to him and enhance his kingdom. More often, though, God prompts feedback from our students so that we will know, at least in part, that lives are being affected.

The most obvious way we know students are listening and believing is that they begin to put into practice what we profess. For example: The subject of forgiveness was on my heart for several months and, no matter the topic at hand, the application of forgiveness kept creeping into many of the lessons I taught. One morning as I talked about the need for us to forgive those who have wronged us, a hand shot up. Donna stated, "There is no way I will ever forgive the man who hurt me. I would be happy to see him run over by a truck!"

We, of course, had some interchange in class with other students expressing sympathy, but all agreeing that forgiveness would have to happen eventually if Donna was to become the woman God had in mind for her to be. I caught up with her after class and asked if she wanted to talk further. She did not.

Over the next several months, I kept teaching on various subjects, and the topic of forgiveness kept coming up, often as a sidelight, but always there—and Donna kept faithfully attending class and participating in the assignments and discussions. But, during this time, she was struggling in other areas of her life, primarily in her physical and emotional health. She really did want to grow spiritually, though, and finally admitted that she knew she needed to forgive this man, but she didn't think she could do it. My wise, prayer warrior friend Marge Lembke and I offered to meet with her and to pray with her. She said she would think about it.

Weeks passed. We continued to meet as a class, study God's Word, and discuss various applications to our lives. One day after class, Donna approached Marge, and said she was ready to meet. The three of us scheduled a time, we sat together, we talked, we allowed Donna to vent her anger, and then we spent time praying over her and with her. She agreed that, to the best of her ability and with the help of the Holy Spirit for what she could not do on her own, she was making the choice to forgive the person who had hurt her so deeply. She left that day with a smile on her face—something we had not seen for a long time.

A couple of weeks later, I mentioned in our class that sometimes we have to forgive someone over and over again. Forgiveness of a deep hurt is a process, not a once-and-for-all action. She came up after class and said, "I know exactly what you mean. I keep having to remind myself that I have forgiven him. But I am doing it—over and over again. Someday I hope I won't have to remind myself so often." There were tears in her eyes, but she was still smiling.

Did I feel that the teaching I was doing resulted in a changed life? You bet. The change I saw in Donna has been real and lasting and one that I could not have imagined after her first outburst of anger against the person who had hurt her. She is a developing person, more complete, more in tune with God's will for her life, and more able to grow up spiritually. An encouragement like that will keep me going for a long time! Those of you who teach know exactly what I mean.

Another time, my husband and I counseled a dear friend whose marriage was in big trouble. He was consumed by a feeling of helplessness because his wife had moved out of their home and he was fearful that she was gone from him forever. He couldn't sleep at night or focus on his very demanding business during the day. He could think of little else other than the uncertainty of their future together, the pain he was experiencing, and the helplessness he felt.

We suggested that he simply give the entire situation over to God. He said he had done that, but it kept coming back. He couldn't seem to escape the emotional turmoil in which he found himself. We then suggested that he give the situation back to God again and again and again until it became a habit simply to pray the problem to God whenever it entered his mind. We even commented that he may have to do it a hundred times a day at first. Then after a couple of days, maybe it would only be ninety times a day, then eighty, then fifty, until he found that, when he gave it to God, he was no longer trying to take it back and solve the problem himself.

It was pretty simple advice, but in his desperation, he took it. He later told us that, as he walked out our front door, he gave the problem to God—again. Then again and again and again throughout the entire day. For the first time in weeks, he slept well that night. He began to regain perspective, to let go of trying to control the situation, to give his wife freedom to make decisions, to pray again about other things, and to experience the peace that passes human understanding.

When someone listens to your teaching or wisdom that you have gleaned from Scripture and applies it effectively in their lives, you know that you are connecting. In our friend's case, it took a long time for his wife to choose to come back home, but she did. Neither my advice nor my husband's could fix the marriage. God could. But our friend first had to give the situation over to him. Then God could work in his heart and in the heart of his wife in order to begin to mend the brokenness of their relationship. And while that was happening, he was getting rest, focusing on other issues in his life, and growing in relationship with God.

God's approval is our highest reward as teachers, but watching lives transform comes a close second. I am grateful for every student whose life is affected in either a small or big way and who communicates that change back to me. Their feedback energizes me and compels me to stay tuned to the Holy Spirit, to stay focused on God's Word, and to teach my heart out!

In this chapter we will explore several methods that will help us to connect with our students with the greatest possible impact. But, before we do that, let's take a look at what some of our master teachers have to say about preparing and presenting our lessons in such a way that real, life-changing connection can be made with those who listen:

I try to share how the Lord has used Scripture in my own life, without preaching about myself. To present Jesus in the Word is to give them the answer they need.

—Dr. Warren Wiersbe

I use a grid of four steps in every presentation: identification, translation, persuasion, and justification. I must be able to identify with the needs and struggles of the audience. Then it should be God's truth in their idiom. Thirdly, there should be persuasive elements in style and content. Finally, the assertions made that are expecting a response should be justified by truth support and not just stated glibly.

—Dr. Ravi Zacharias

In my classroom, I began every class with Scripture, which is the written Word, the center of our faith. The written Word (a Book, words on a page) affirms our teaching and our passion. Beginning every class with Scripture naturally led into unpackaging verses, meditating on them, peeling off the layers, and seeing how they applied to what we were looking at in class that day. I began to see how we integrate spiritual truths into our academic disciplines.

—Jo Kadlecek

It is very important to present the truth of God's Word with relevance, but not to the point where we culturally contextualize our message so that we avoid uncomfortable, unpopular subjects or that we water down things to the extent that there is no sense of conviction … Doctrine and duty, belief and behavior go hand-in-hand and are really inseparable.

—Rev. William Dondit

I desire that my students seek to go out into a culture that desperately needs that message of love and grace and are able to present that message in winsome ways that will invite others to want to know more about who Jesus is and why his claims on our lives are so revolutionary.

—Dr. Ron Mahurin

I tell young preachers that every sermon should answer these questions: "What burning issues are you answering that people should be asking?" and "After you are finished, would people feel free to come and discuss the topic with you?" and "Why should anyone's life be changed forever because of this message or teaching?"

—Dr. Erwin Lutzer

In each class it is my goal to teach the lesson (the "what?"), help them to see the significance (the "so what?"), and encourage them to make application of the lesson to their lives (the "now what?").

—Dr. Tamara Rosier

Gleaning from these comments and from our own experience, let's explore some tried-and-true methods of connecting effectively with those whom we teach.

- Personal experience. In his book, *Teaching to Change Lives*, Howard Hendricks says, "What you *are* is far more important than what you say or do. God's method is always incarnational. He loves to take his truth and wrap it in a person" (p. 74). If our goal is to impart truth, the most credible way to achieve the goal is to show how that truth has affected us. If we have not learned personally the lesson we are teaching, our teaching will be flat and lifeless. On the other hand, if we can tell our classes how the truth of what we are teaching has changed us or helped us, our teaching will become real and effective. Master teacher Nataly Berckmann illustrates this when she says that, as she matured as a human being and in her own relationships, she became a better teacher:

My teaching skills developed partly through raising my own two children. I learned a lot about their differences. They have differing abilities, differing desires, and differing gifts. My children were different from me and their differences gave me new perspectives that I take into the classroom.

Our students need to know that we are real people. We are not super-saints. We have our own struggles to overcome and our own growing to do. It is important that we tell our stories. I write a monthly newsletter that I distribute through my website. A couple of months ago, I wrote about the death of my father, much as I have recounted in the Introduction of this book. I received more feedback on that newsletter than on any other. Why? Because I told a real story from my life and, through it, forged a connection between my readers and me. If they had lost a parent, they understood. If they had not, they sympathized. But my humanity touched them. All of our stories, if they are real and told with sincerity, will do that. We must not be fearful of letting our students know the real people we are. Master teacher Jo Kadlecek puts it this way:

One thing I have really learned is the power of story. We are living in an age when we don't want just people talking at us. We want stories. That is the best way to learn. There is something mysterious and powerful and inherent about stories to humans. If we were to try to recount to each other what our pastors said last Sunday, we probably couldn't do it, but I could tell you some of the stories he told us. There is something intriguing about story and the power of story in teaching. The best qualification for teachers of the Word is their ability to use story to help communicate things. Along with that is their willingness to be honest, real and personal about their communication. If our own story is not integrated into the story of Scripture, we will not be as effective as teachers.

- Relevance. The only way our teaching will be relevant is if we make a concerted effort to know our audience and what resonates with them. If they are teens, our message will be delivered differently than if they are senior citizens. Teachers must become skilled at keeping the content of the message the same, always the truth of the Word of God, but changing its style or "feeling" so that our listeners will be able to understand and apply it. How do we do that? One way is to be constantly reading and learning the same information that is being accessed by our students. Here is what one of our master teachers says about this matter:

Teachers have to be students of two worlds: The world of the Bible and the world in which we live. I spend time studying culture through media, magazines, and interactions with key leaders through their writing. At the same time, I study

Scripture. My job as a minister is to bridge the two by bringing in appropriate application of scriptural concepts to my teaching.

—Dr. Don Denyes

If we teach teens, we should have an awareness of the music they listen to, the celebrities they admire, the kinds of things they are studying in the classroom, and the social issues that influence or disturb them. This takes time and effort on our part, but we will be teaching into the wind if we are not aware of what is going on in the minds, hearts, and lives of our listeners. This may be easier if we are teaching people who are "like us." However, if we are middle-aged or older and are teaching newlyweds, younger parents, or career-focused young couples, we need to listen to them, be attuned to their needs, and adjust our teaching accordingly. A ready audience is a key component to successful teaching. We sense what they are ready to receive by first figuring out what they care about, struggle with, and need—and then teach to those needs.

A second component of relevance is finding *stories and illustrations* that will touch the minds and hearts of students. Jesus was a master at making great spiritual truths relevant to his audiences. He did this primarily by first meeting their physical needs and then by telling stories that arose from life experiences they understood. We can do the same.

A third part of relevance is *teaching style*. Cornerstone University president Rex Rogers explains that he uses a very traditional style of going through the Bible verse by verse or concept by concept with the senior adults he teaches. They like that method because they are accustomed to it. They have always been taught that way and they learn best that way. Trying to engage them in discussion is never very fruitful. However, Dr. Rogers went on to say that, when he teaches college students, his teaching is more effective if he primes their thinking by some teaching and then throws out some concepts for them to consider and discuss. He guides the discussion, of course, but allows them freedom to think through the issue and express their thoughts and ideas on the subject. They go away from his classes with their brains stimulated and their hearts pondering the ideas presented. They would not respond as well to having to sit through an hour-long lecture approach to teaching.

- Individual attention. We must never underestimate the power of one contact, one word, one touch, or one conversation in the life of a student. I had a friend early in my career who taught high school with me. She had five classes every day, each consisting of twenty-five or thirty students. At the beginning of each new class hour, she would survey the

> We must never underestimate the power of one contact, one word, one touch, or one conversation in the life of a student.

faces of the high schoolers sitting in front of her and would determine who needed a special word that day. As the class filed out, she always found one student whom she made to feel special by a compliment or an encouraging word. I have often thought about her habit of building significance into the lives of her students simply by saying the right word at the right time to the right person. The students in her classes were not just bodies sitting in rows. They were real human beings with personalities and needs and, by her actions, they knew that she saw them as individuals.

In his book, *A Listening Ear*, noted Swiss physician Paul Tournier tells the story of his life being transformed by a teacher's simple act:

When I was sixteen, one of my teachers must have guessed that this odd young boy needed someone to hold out a friendly hand to him, and he made a quite unprecedented gesture. He invited me to his home. That was my first encounter. I was embarrassed and overawed as I went into his small study, its walls covered with bookshelves from floor to ceiling. I did not know what to say. Later on I realized that in all probability he did not know what to say either, but he did something vitally important for me. Through him I began to exist. I was no longer a pupil in front of a teacher, but a person in front of a person (p. 19).

Orphaned by the age of six and was raised by an aunt and uncle, Tournier describes deep feelings of insecurity as an adolescent. Looking back on those years, he remembers isolation and aloneness. By the time he was sixteen, his insecurity was at its deepest. Then a teacher came along who sensed a need in him and reached out to give him some personal recognition. Just look at the results.

Tournier went on to become a noted physician and founder of a school of practice that he called "medicine of the person". One of the earliest holistic approaches to caring for patients, it combined medical knowledge, human understanding, and spirituality to heal the whole person. He engaged in this work for more than fifty years in Geneva, Switzerland and wrote sixteen books that have been translated into sixteen languages and have sold approximately 2 million copies. How different his life might have been if he had not received that attention from a teacher when he needed it most.

It is only when we can be "a person in front of a person" with our students that we really connect with them. That can be done only one at a time. As committed teachers, though, we look for opportunities to say the right word and then we look for opportunities for the longer conversations and, perhaps, even meetings outside of the classroom or discussion group. If you have a receptive student, these touches can be life-changing.

- Student questions. In our next chapter, we will talk in more detail about leading good discussions. As a preface to that, I mention briefly here the importance of enabling our students to respond to the message we are presenting before they leave the classroom. There are several methods for doing this. Some teachers prefer to present material at the beginning the class in a lecture or lecture/discussion format, then to conclude with time to spare in order to allow the class to ask questions about the material presented. If we are going to allow for questions, we are wise to let our audience know that at the beginning of our presentation. Knowing they will have an opportunity to response encourages them to be mentally engaged during the lecture phase of our presentation.

In opening the floor for discussion, you risk being asked a question you either don't want to answer (perhaps because it is a side issue not directly relevant to the message you want your students to leave with) or cannot answer because you simply don't know. Don't panic. Remember that you are the teacher and, therefore, you are in control of the situation. If you think a question is not relevant, simply defer it and ask the student to bring it to you outside of the classroom so that you can discuss it one-on-one (this could be a great connection opportunity) or ask him to raise it in class at a time when it is more relevant to the topic at hand. You are not required to answer every question that is posed.

If you are asked a question for which you do not know the answer, simply say so. Then ask if someone else in the class would like to respond. Or offer to research the question and bring an answer at the next meeting. If your teaching is a one-time presentation, offer to e-mail the questioner with your answer after you have a chance to do some reading on the topic. Last, realize that not all questions have answers.

- Assignments. When we are teaching classes that meet on an ongoing basis, carefully crafted assignments sometimes provide the best possible way for students to think over and then respond to our teaching. For my Saturday morning group, I think long and hard before I make up the assignment for the following week because I know that the questions that my students take home to answer will often determine whether the lesson has a transforming effect in their lives.

I try to include a few questions that revisit the content of the week's lesson. Those questions serve as a guide for review of the material when we meet the following week for discussion. Then I include a few questions that require personal application. They may ask for students to ponder experiences in their lives that relate to the lesson, or to evaluate what personal growth may need to occur relative to the topic at hand, or to think of ways to apply the lesson as they go about their lives in the coming week. Often I conclude with a prayer or meditation exercise, enabling students to progress from truth to application to transformation.

When we meet the following Saturday, we discuss the assignment from the previous week before we launch into the new lesson material. I have been amazed time and again at how the assignment questions have stimulated new thoughts or reactions from students. Those thoughts broaden them, for certain, but the bonus is that they broaden my thinking and understanding as well.

- Evaluations. OK, this is scary. We all admit to being afraid to ask students to evaluate our teaching, but the benefits will most certainly far outweigh any results that make us uncomfortable. When asking students for evaluations, we should make sure that we provide them with specific questions to answer, that we make their responses anonymous, and that we assure them that they can be totally honest. Our goal, we must remember, is to teach effectively. The message we have is important and life changing. We are teaching to honor God above all. His evaluation is ultimately the one that really counts. But, he can teach us through those we teach. We just have to be willing to ask. Most of them respond in great gentleness!

Master teacher Jo Kadlecek captures the essence of teaching with true connection this way:

I think the best teachers are those who love what they are teaching. Then it becomes contagious. When we see a great work of art or beauty, we immediately want to show someone else. To me, that is a form of teaching. It is the kernel behind every great teaching moment.

 ## Let's Review and Evaluate

How are we doing as we attempt to improve our connections with students?

Do we make sincere eye contact as we speak, to ensure that there is person-to-person communication?

Do we receive feedback from our students that indicates specific lessons have been understood and applied?

Do we provide our students with ways to give us such feedback by assignments, evaluation opportunities, and our accessibility?

Do we make time to connect one-on-one with students who have special needs or who show particular interest?

Talking without connecting is not teaching. True teaching occurs only when the students have received the message and have applied it in ways that change them for eternity.

SIX

LEADING GOOD DISCUSSIONS

*If you want to change a person permanently,
make sure his thinking changes, and not merely his behavior.*

—Howard Hendricks in *Teaching to Change Lives*

This chapter provides the following pointers on how to lead a good discussion:

- Introducing the topic in a way that will entice interaction.
- Listening creatively to the conversation.
- Handling interrupters and distracters.
- Keeping the focus and moving toward conclusion.
- Reviewing for emphasis and remembering.

There are many learning formats and teaching techniques that can be used in various educational arenas. We all learn in different ways and, as teachers, we acknowledge those differences in learning styles and need to provide as many differing kinds of learning opportunities as possible. Dr. Tamara Rosier reminds us, "We must not be afraid of the mystery of learning." But, whatever method a teacher uses primarily, all experienced teachers agree that interaction with students is a requirement if true, long-term, life-changing learning is to occur.

Discussion is one way in which some students learn best. These learners like to interact with the concepts that are being taught, to roll the ideas around in their minds, and then test their conclusions by interacting with their peers. This method is helpful to teachers because, through discussion, we can really tell if we are engaging the minds and hearts of our students. Even though we stand in front of the class and teach with authority conferred on us by God, we are equal to our students as members of the Body of Christ, not superior to them. They, too, have the indwelling Holy Spirit to enlighten them and to give insights that he may not be giving to us. In a healthy, well run discussion format, both teachers and students become learners.

Master teachers have found discussion and student interaction to be essential in effective teaching. Here are some of their techniques and insights:

I present a lot of "what if's" to my students. These help them to think through situations and come up with solutions that make sense. I ask students to tell me what they are struggling with. Then we search together to see what God says about it.

—Kathleen O. Sindorf

First I study the subject, then I move toward interaction with those I am teaching. Feedback can help me to adjust my style or approach to make sure I connect. Even though I have been schooled by great lecturers, I enjoy the interactive approach of teaching.

—Dr. Rex Rogers

Relationships are very important in my classroom. Teaching is relationship and leadership. Everything I learned about leadership I learned in the classroom. I really believe that a teacher is a facilitator, especially in teaching the Bible. We learn together. Sometimes I set up a problem for students to work on or a scenario to react to. I try to talk less in class and get the students to talk to each other and to me. With a feeling of safety, they will talk and will begin to tap into what each of them knows.

—Dr. Tamara Rosier

I lecture, but I also like to dialogue with students. When I teach, I absolutely need interaction. I believe that all teachers and preachers have to have what I call "connectedness"; that is, they need to connect with people if they want to communicate. It is not enough to give out content, there must be transformation, and you can only do that when you win the person over to yourself. If they like you, they will learn. If they don't it doesn't matter much how great your lectures are.

—Dr. Erwin Lutzer

I am very much drawn to the notion that Scripture must be learned in community. I find that in many (though thankfully, not all) evangelical settings we have become preoccupied with our individual relationship with God, to the detriment of the body of Christ and the engagement of the broader culture. In teaching God's Word, I want to draw the listener into that space and place where they must wrestle with the realities of the brokenness of our world, and at the same time, the loving grace that God extends to us in Christ.

—Dr. Ron Mahurin

One method that I have used is to form a feedback group to whom I would deliver the gist of the teaching prior to my completion of preparation. I then ask, "How does this touch your world?" Their responses guide the way I complete and present the sermon.

—Dr. Don Denyes

I recently showed a short video in class about a man who gave a birthday party for a prostitute. I asked the class to think about how many of them would have been willing to do that, and then I asked them how many of them would see Jesus doing such a thing. The discussion told me that they understood that Jesus is our model and sometimes the things he would do might be out of our comfort zone, but that doesn't mean we shouldn't extend ourselves to do them. The discussion told me that they had connected with the message of the video.

—Kathleen O. Sindorf

The Master Teacher Model

Learning from earthly master teachers is very helpful, but in this chapter, we are going to turn for direction to the greatest Master Teacher of all: Jesus himself. It is clear from Scripture that Jesus was considered to be an amazing teacher. In fact, in Matthew 7:28 and 29 we are told, "When Jesus had finished saying these things, the crowds were amazed at his teaching, because he taught as one who had authority, and not as their teachers of the law." So he was called "rabbi" or "teacher" or "master" by both friends and enemies, titles that were given out of respect for what he knew and how he taught. Most rabbis quoted extensively from the law, prophets, and writings. Jesus was no exception. They also referred often to interpretations of the law that had been written by other rabbis and commonly accepted to be valid. The truly gifted rabbis, however, offered their own wisdom and interpretation, as Jesus did in a way that was revolutionary.

In Jesus's day Jewish boys were taught the Torah in the synagogue until age fifteen. At that age, many of the young men began their working life, but truly dedicated students of the law might choose to study with a respected rabbi and become his disciple. Rabbis became adept at teaching by storytelling, at leading dynamic discussions, at seeing object lessons on every journey, and in helping their students uncover truths from what they already knew. Such was the case with Jesus and his closest followers. Jesus was unique, however, in that his disciples did not choose him; rather, he chose them. He specifically called out twelve men to be taught by him, twelve men who would listen, observe, and absorb all he could teach them in the short time he had remaining in his earthly life, twelve men who, for the most part were not scholars themselves but humble, uneducated Galileans.

In the rabbinical tradition, Jesus's band of disciples lived with him, worked with him, traveled with him, and lived life with him, learning all they could from the eternal wisdom and knowledge he possessed. As they worked and ate together, many questions were raised by the students, wise teaching was given by the Rabbi, and, often, lively discussion ensued.

As we might expect, there was no one who led better discussions than Jesus did, and many of his conversations with his disciples, with seekers, and with the religious leaders are recorded in the pages of the Bible for our benefit. I think one of the best model discussions we can emulate as we engage with our students is found in the Gospel of John, Chapters 13 through 16. In these chapters, Jesus is meeting with his closest followers for the last time before he will be betrayed, tried, and killed. In retrospect, we can see how important these final words of Jesus were; but, for the disciples, it was a discussion like many they had had with him throughout the previous several years. Their obvious comfort in asking him questions and engaging in free interchange with him tells us that they were used to this format, that they trusted their teacher, and that they knew if they asked sincere questions, he would give them honest and insightful answers. Wouldn't it be great if the same could be said of us?

How did he do it? I've studied Jesus's example for many years now, and tried in my own humanly limited way to emulate him. I've distilled what I've learned into what I hope is a useful and memorable model for you. In the remainder of this chapter, I outline the three things that Jesus brought to his teaching:

Methods

Message

Mindset

And the six things he did as a teacher, which we, as his followers who are teachers, can emulate:

Link

Learn

Launch

Listen

Lead

Look

Let's take a closer look at this model together.

- Methods. Jesus used several teaching methods in leading this prolonged discussion. To convey his message, he used object lessons, parables, lectures, questions and answers—and he even taught in a variety of settings, and when other things were going on, always seizing the teachable moment with his students.

- **Message.** Jesus's primary message was that things were about to change dramatically for his followers. He was going to be betrayed, he was going to leave them for a time, the Holy Spirit would come, they needed to keep trusting him, they would be persecuted, and eventually they would be permanently reunited with him. It was a more difficult and obscure (to the listeners, that is) message than any we ever will have to teach. Because so much was changing and so much was "other worldly," the disciples really did not understand all that he was teaching until after the events of the next few days took place.

- **Mindset.** It was obvious in this interchange that Jesus's primary concern was the well-being of his students. He had an important message to get across and was willing to adjust to meet them where they were in order to bring them along step-by-step to the understanding he needed to have them reach. His mind was set on the events that were about to happen and on making sure that his followers would understand. As to the mindset of his listeners, it is equally obvious that they felt comfortable with him. They could ask questions about what they did not understand and know that he would respond in kindness and clarity. They were genuinely interested in what he had to say and had a strong desire to latch onto the message he was giving them.

How do we follow in the footsteps of this Master Teacher as we, too, try to convey a message by effectively leading discussions?

- **Link.** For Jesus, preparing to teach, I believe, was entirely focused on his relationship with his Father. He even says so in John 14: 24b, "These words you hear are not my own; they belong to the Father who sent me." This is part of the reason that Jesus spent great periods of time in prayer. He was receiving his instructions and his message from his Father in heaven.

"... but the world must learn that I love the Father and that I do exactly what my Father has commanded me" (14:31). If we learn nothing else from Jesus's teaching style (although I believe there is *much* else to learn!), connection with the Father might be the most important habit we can adopt.

The power in our teaching comes from our link with God through the indwelling Holy Spirit who brings things to our minds, softens our hearts, and gives us insight into spiritual issues. It would be frightening to try to lead a discussion on matters of eternal significance without this vital link to our ultimate resource and enlightenment.

- Learn. As with all teaching, we teach best if we are well prepared. Of course, Jesus didn't have the problem of learning his material, but we, in our finiteness, have that obstacle to face. Scholarly preparation may be even more important in leading discussions than it is in a lecture approach. Why? Because when we open concepts up to students for feedback, we never know what we are going to get from them. We have to be always prepared to field questions, respond to new directions in thinking, and encourage open minds and hearts. So, when we prepare to discuss a topic in a group setting, we must know the topic well. We prepare by studying the scriptural texts or texts that relate, reading all we can that is relevant to the issue at hand, and then sitting with our thoughts for awhile, mulling, stewing, and pondering all the various aspects of the issue. With the help of good resources and the enlightenment of the Holy Spirit, we will be ready to guide our students into effective and life-changing discussion on the subject at hand.

- Launch. Waking up the minds of our students is essential if we want good discussion to ensue. Jesus did that very effectively when, before they even began to eat their meal together, he took a towel and a basin of water and washed their feet. The foot washing scene that is described in John 13 was an object lesson used by Jesus for two purposes:

1. To teach his disciples the importance of daily cleansing. All but one of them (Jesus pointed out that there was one who was not fully clean) had experienced the total, eternal cleansing that comes by believing in him and, thereby, becoming a regenerated child of God. Jesus pointed out in his conversation with Peter that they did not need that overall cleansing ever again. But they *did* need the daily cleansing of their feet, and he stooped before each of them to perform that task for them. His dialogue with Peter made it clear that his washing of his disciples' feet was a way for him to create an indelible image in their minds, reminding them of their need to go to him from that day forward every time they were contaminated with sin in their lives. It would happen as long as they were living in this world, and Jesus lives today to hear our confession and cleanse our sins (I John 1:9).

2. To model for his students the concept of being a servant. People in those days wore open sandals and walked just about everywhere they went. The climate was hot and the roads were dusty and dirty. When guests arrived at someone's home, a servant (usually the lowliest servant in the household) was sent in to wash their feet. In the case of Jesus and his disciples, they were meeting for a meal in a borrowed room. There was no host or servant to take care of them. None of the disciples volunteered for the lowly task of washing each other's dirty feet. But Jesus did. And he is clear in his teaching at the end of the foot washing that he expected them to follow his example and be servants to each other.

This dramatic object lesson captured their attention, I am sure, and their attention was what Jesus wanted because he had much to teach them on this very important evening.

When we prepare to lead a discussion, we should think about how we will introduce the topic in a way that will cause our students to get immediately involved. What can we do in terms of an object lesson, a story, an illustration, or a personal experience that will stimulate participants to thinking bigger thoughts and to engaging spiritual concepts? Before we open our group discussion, we should think about what it is that we want our students to walk away with when our time together is over. The attention grabber and/or thought stimulator that we use at the beginning of our discussion should center around that theme so that the initial discussion will be on point. We may talk around it in a hundred different ways before the discussion has been completed, but, as leaders, we want to begin and end on the primary point of the lesson. As mentioned earlier, we never want our students to walk away thinking, "What was *that* all about?"

Jesus wanted his disciples to think about two main points: The first was cleansing (he reiterates this in the parable of the vine and the branches in John, Chapter 15) and the second was following his example. Later in this same discussion, he talks about the Holy Spirit coming to remind them of everything he had taught them. He wanted his disciples to model their lives after him and his teaching. Serving each other was a very important part of that modeling. So, we find that Jesus's introductory object lesson became the foundation for the teaching and discussion that would follow for the rest of the evening.

Another preliminary step in launching a good discussion might be to have students prepare for the conversation prior to the meeting. When I am teaching on ongoing series of lessons, for example, I will give an assignment to be completed prior to coming the next week. That way, we can begin each class with discussion of the assignment. This serves as a review of the material presented the week before and prepares us for the new lesson to be given that day. If the students have carefully reviewed and worked out the discussion questions ahead of time, their contributions to the interaction are more valuable and well thought out. Any questions they bring are more likely to be apropos to the subject at hand. And a real bonus for me, as the teacher, is that Spirit-led students will, without doubt, bring back to the discussion new insights that they have received during the week as they dug into Scripture to prepare for our time together.

- Listen. All through Chapters 13–16 of John, Jesus teaches, but he also listens. He fields questions and comments specifically from Peter, John, Judas Iscariot, Thomas, Philip, and the other disciple also named Judas. John does not record every bit of the discussion among Jesus and his disciples, but he gives us enough specifics to allow us to understand that this was not a sermon, it was an interchange. Jesus taught, to be sure, but he did not deliver a one-sided lecture. He invited questions and comments. He wanted them to understand, so he patiently dealt with each question as it was raised. As long as they were asking questions, he could tell if they were tracking with him. He could know if he needed to backtrack to pick up those who had fallen behind. Apparently, during this process, he realized that certain points needed reiteration. For example, he talks to them about his leaving and the coming of the Holy Spirit in Chapter 14 and then again in Chapter 16. He wants to make sure they "get" it. And apparently, the discussion they were having indicated to him that they needed to hear it again.

One of the most important roles of a good discussion leader is active listening. We will hear questions and how we answer those questions will be, in part, the measure of our success as teachers. Dr. Rex Rogers tells the story of one of his own early college professors:

I was bursting with questions about Creation, dinosaurs, prophecy, the flood, TULIP, inspiration, free will, civil religion, the Trinity, nuclear weapons, infant salvation, capitalism, Christian liberty, cultural relativism, modernity, and the number of angels who could fit on a pin. You name it; in Theology 101 I asked it.

I didn't know what to call it then, but I was full of doubts. Not doubt about God's existence—the idea of God never troubled me. But I questioned Christianity and doubted that I really could be saved. My doubts were a combination of a weak faith and a rationalistic mind. I wanted to know if the Christian faith could stand the test of point-blank questions—ones that had rattled my Sunday-school teachers and ones I mistakenly thought would foil my theology professor.

Poor Dr. (Mead) Armstrong was the target for all this youthful curiosity and confusion. Five days a week in that quarter-system class he patiently and thoroughly answered my questions. A seemingly unlimited font of quoted Scripture graced every answer. What I learned in Theology 101 was not another man's opinion but biblical doctrine. I can yet see him quoting Scripture and can still quote many of those verses myself.

What if Dr. Armstrong had simply seen this student as a troublemaker trying to disrupt class with his questions? His responses might have been more abrupt, less scriptural, and less helpful in reinforcing the faith life of young Rex. Instead, he listened between the lines and saw into the heart and mind of a student who was struggling with doubts. He then reinforced the truth of God by quoting from the Bible. After all, we are told that faith comes by hearing the word of God. The result, according to Dr. Rogers's testimony today, is that these discussions between student and teacher changed his life forever. They bolstered his faith and directed his attention to the Bible, which became the passion of his life and career.

In every group, there is someone who may be a challenge to us as discussion leaders.

There is the *monopolizer* who gives 15-minute answers via digression and storytelling. I remember praying once in the middle of a discussion (silently, of course!) reminding God that if he could shut the mouths of lions for Daniel, would he please shut the mouth of one participant who just did not know when to stop talking? Praying might not be the only thing you can do, however. Sometimes you might simply have to interrupt the talker, thank her for her thoughts, and confidently bring the class back to the lesson you are presenting.

Then there is the *free associater* for whom every question raised makes him think of something else that is off the subject. Sometimes free associaters are truly trying to understand; most times, though, it seems that they are simply not tracking with you and need to be reminded kindly of the topic at hand. We have to be very vigilant as shepherds in that case, bringing the entire group gently back to the issues of focus.

Every once in awhile, we run into someone who is an *arguer* and makes his case with anger and zeal. This can poison a classroom. No one wants to come to a Bible study and leave with a churning stomach because of the tension that was caused by an angry student. Arguers need to be handled with firmness and care and, by gentle correction, prevented from clouding the thinking of the entire group. Meeting with the student outside of class may defuse his anger by giving him a forum in which he can present his views to you one-on-one.

The *expert* can be a real challenge. He has a better way of looking at things, will make minor corrections in the teaching (unfortunately he may often be right; we do make mistakes and it seems that there is always an expert who will point them out). The best response is to acknowledge and correct any error we recognize—and then to get the class back on track as quickly as possible. If the expert is simply showing off his own knowledge, let him go briefly and then take control and get back to the lesson in front of you. Remember that you are the teacher, this is your classroom, and you have prepared. In light of all of that, in this time and place, you are the expert. Teach with confidence and authority.

Responding to the *questioner* takes a bit of discernment. Often her questions are truly legitimate and she sincerely wants to learn. In that case, the question deserves a response. If you feel the answer to the question will benefit the entire class, take time to answer it when it is asked. If the question will be dealt with at a later point in the lesson (many times this is the case) or series of lessons, tell the questioner to stay tuned because the topic will come up in scheduled teaching. If you feel the question is not pertinent to where the rest of the class is at the moment, tell the questioner that, while she has raised a valid point, it might be best for the two of you to meet after class to talk about it so that the rest of the class session can be used to complete the discussion at hand. If you can do this while showing respect to the questioner, you will maintain control; and the question, if sincere, will be addressed at the appropriate time.

The *jokester* can actually help to lighten the class, so don't get too distraught over the quips or comments that arise as long as they are not put downs of you or one of the students. We often take ourselves too seriously, so a comic in the class will help to relieve the tension of a deep subject and will help to keep the class lively. If it gets out of hand, however, you may need to talk to the quipper after class and see if you can get him on your side in terms of keeping the focus on the teaching you have prepared. If that doesn't work, simply smile at the comment made and keep moving through your teaching. Once the class sees you are not buying into the interruptive humor, eventually peer pressure will help to control the jokester.

Perhaps one of the greatest challenges to leading a discussion and listening to students is drawing in the *nonparticipator*. In every class there is a student (or students) who takes notes, listens with rapt attention, follows the discussion, and never says a word. I have found that these still waters often do run deep, so if we can draw this student out, we may find incredible insight. One way to get her to talk is to ask her a question directly. Make it a simple one so that she can answer correctly, then affirm the response. Or ask her to read a Scripture verse or passage you are teaching from. If she hears her voice out loud she may realize that, nothing terrible happened when she spoke and gain confidence in her ability to contribute. If the nonparticipator does not become more responsive, though, don't fret. All personalities are different, and some are just quieter than others. As teachers, we must make sure all are welcome to participate, all are given opportunity to enter into discussion without being drowned out by others, and all participants are treated with respect. After that, the response is up to the individual student. The more participation the better, but you don't need 100-percent participation to consider yourself a success.

We must make sure all are welcome to participate, all are given opportunity to enter into discussion without being drowned out by others, and all participants are treated with respect.

- Lead. As you will conclude from the discussion above, leading good discussions means exercising both wisdom and patience as we gently instruct and carefully lead those who are in our group. We walk a very narrow path of needing to control the flow of discussion, but, at the same time, knowing that we do not want to control our students' thoughts. Exercising appropriate leadership will enable the discussion to be genuine, free, and open without having the atmosphere charged with tension or stilted by a few class members who wish to disagree, digress, dominate, or divert. By learning to listen to our students and responding to their heart needs instead of just their surface comments or questions, we will be able to pick them up where they are and lead them to the next level in our teaching. What does a good discussion leader do to enable this learning process to occur? Jesus is our model here, too.

1. First, he offered variety in activity, place, and method of teaching so that he did not lose the attention of the group. He washed their feet, teaching as he did so and, thus, provided the foundation for the teaching that would follow and a visual image of what he meant by cleansing and by humble service. Then they sat down

(or reclined as was common in Middle Eastern cultures of the day) and ate a meal together. While they ate, he taught them and responded to their requests for clarification (specifically, they were curious as to whom it was Jesus was referring when he said that one of them would betray him). He continued to teach them about the onslaught that he was about to undergo. He told them he would be leaving them, but that the Holy Spirit would be sent to dwell inside of them. Then he suggested that they go for a walk.

As they walked, he taught them lessons from the vine and the branches. We can imagine that they perhaps were walking past a vineyard and he pointed at the branches, some of which were producing luscious grapes and others that were obviously dead and lifeless. He warned them again that evil was coming and that they would be persecuted. He talked to them about how they should treat one another in his absence and he repeated his promise that the Counselor would come in the person of the Holy Spirit.

2. He tested them often to make sure they were following what it was that he was trying to teach. They washed, they ate, they walked, and, all the while, they talked. Jesus taught, they listened and responded, and he answered, taking them always to the next lesson or the next point. At times he repeated what he said probably because the message was so important that he didn't want them to miss it—and perhaps also because there were things he was teaching that they were not quite comprehending. Jesus had an advantage over us as teachers, of course, in that he could read their minds. He knew exactly where they were in their thinking at all times. We have to practice the fine art of mind reading, too, but for us it will always be an inexact science!

3. He created an atmosphere in which free interchange could take place. He took whatever questions they asked and responded to them with care and honesty. He did gently call to account one disciple who asked that Jesus show him the Father because he thought that by now this student should have been catching

on to what he had been teaching them all these years. This tells us that a loving confrontation in a discussion group is acceptable, but we should be sparing and purposeful in our use of that technique. No one will be able to do it as perfectly as Jesus did! Generally, we sense that Jesus was open to any sincere question or comment that his disciples raised, and his openness encouraged their free interchange.

A summary of vital leadership qualities we might want to keep in mind as we shepherd good discussion include these:

Conflict resolution

Helping group members resolve conflicts that may arise. There will be times when our students do not see eye to eye on a particular topic. In that case, our role is to give each party an opportunity to express opinions, point to Scripture as our source for truth, and allow for the fact that, by God's grace, differences of opinion may exist peacefully together.

Focus

Ensuring that comments and questions stay focused on the subject matter at hand. As someone once said, this may be like herding cats. If you have a talkative group, it is easy for sharp minds to wander into new thoughts. As the cat-herder, your job is to acknowledge the interesting aspects of the new thoughts that are brought in, but, then gently steer the discussion back to the topic of focus.

Forward motion

By refocusing the group now and then, by summarizing where we have been in the discussion so far, and by asking leading questions, we keep the group moving toward the teaching goals that we have in mind. Someone has to be the one to keep the conversation on track and moving in the direction of understanding. As leaders, we are the ones to monitor the flow of ideas and to direct them to the desired ends.

If our attention is on these three goals, we will go far in enabling our students to learn by participatory discussion. If we lose sight of these Jesus-modeled techniques, we will lost sight of the teaching that we had intended when we opened the discussion in the first place.

- **Look Back.** Because discussions can sometimes wander down some sideroads (that is not necessarily a negative, as long as we keep bringing the thoughts back to the main road), we must recap for our students, near the conclusion of the discussion, the main points of the lesson that have been explored. We do not want them to leave with random thoughts toppling over one another. Instead, we should return to our opening illustration or example and tie together the threads of the discussion to the primary lesson we intended to teach. That way, they will leave our group with the main goal in mind even as they process the multiple aspects of it that were discussed during the time together. We simply want to ensure that they understand the intended lesson and know how to apply it.

- **Look Up.** Once again, Jesus is our example here. We have been given three chapters in which are records of Jesus's teaching his disciples through discussion and interaction and then bringing that teaching to conclusion with words of warning and words of encouragement. Now, at the beginning of Chapter 17, we are told, "After Jesus said this, he looked toward heaven and prayed." Remember that before he taught, he prayed. Now, after the teaching has concluded, he prays again. His look is always upward, always toward the Father. He looks to God for direction, for words, for understanding, for protection, and for completion of the work that is to be done in this world. How would we dare to do less?

I have found it very beneficial (a) in building a strong group dynamic, (b) in putting into practice the lessons that we learn, and (c) in practicing reliance on the power of God in our lives to conclude discussion or teaching sessions with a time of prayer. Sometimes we will share requests and spend some time interceding for one another. At other times, we will approach God in quietness and spend time in listening prayer, waiting for his voice or his direction. Whatever the method we choose, the result is that we leave our group focused on God. With prayer as our concluding activity, we leave the place prepared for whatever may come. For Jesus, it was arrest, trial, and death. But his focus was upward and, with that focus, he could face anything. So can we. So can our students.

 Let's Review and Evaluate

How are we doing in the discussion arena?

Are we open to the opinions of others or are we pretty certain we have all the answers?

Do we encourage open discussion and free expression of opinions among our students?

Are we well enough prepared in our topic that we are able to field questions with biblically based answers?

Are we able to successfully guide a discussion to a conclusion that teaches a scriptural principle?

What specific thing can we do to improve our ability to lead strongly interactive discussions?

If we can learn to lead stimulating discussions, our classes will be bursting at the seams. Learning today is participatory. Students do not want to be told everything they need to know. Instead, they want to learn *how* to learn. They want to explore new ideas and come to their own conclusions. They want to be actively involved in the learning process.

Carefully crafted and guided discussions by teachers who think deeply and engage creatively will encourage such involvement by students. And students' lives are more likely to be changed by something they discover through free-flowing discussion than by anything we simply tell them.

SEVEN

ONE-ON-ONE MENTORING

> Christianity wants to grant the single individual
> eternal happiness, a good that is not distributed
> in bulk but only to one, and to one at a time.
>
> —Soren Kierkegaard in *Provocations*

In this chapter, we will explore:

- Determining whether you should be a mentor.
- Designing a plan for one-on-one mentoring.
- Following a plan to achieve the results you desire.
- Finding a mentor for your own areas of need.

Darla and I sat in the coffee shop and she began to talk. Her life, she thought, should be better than it was. She had a faithful husband, healthy children, a beautiful home, and financial security, but she was unhappy. She felt inadequate and ineffective. It seemed that life was making demands of her that she could not fulfill to her own satisfaction and, often, to the satisfaction of her husband and children.

"Can you teach me how to live my life?" she asked.

That was a pretty big question, and I knew it would be an even bigger assignment if I chose to take it on. I knew that what she really was looking for was a mentor. Could I be that person for her? I, at first, felt flattered that she would look at my life and think that I was capable and confident and, therefore, able to help her live her own life better. Then, I felt underqualified. Who was I to think that I could counsel another woman as to how her life should be lived? I left the coffee shop thanking her for her request and telling her that I needed time to pray about it and seek God's direction before I gave her an answer.

That was four years ago. Since then, Darla and I have met periodically and have gone through a mentoring program that I wrote specifically for her. We met weekly at first, then every other week, and now we are at a point where we touch base for lunch now and then. It has been an interesting journey for both of us and one in which we both learned a great deal about each other, about God's individual leading in our lives, and about how we can draw on another human being for strength and wisdom.

While Darla has been my longest term mentee, there have been numerous others with whom I have had ongoing dialogues and meetings to serve as a sounding board and an advisor for some of life's troublesome issues.

It is one thing to stand in front of a class and teach a lesson or lead a discussion and quite another to provide one-on-one mentoring for an individual. I have found mentoring to be more demanding of me personally, emotionally, and spiritually than group teaching. One-on-one relationships get to the core of another person and to the core of my own soul. There are frustrations when the mentee doesn't just automatically put into practice what we have taught or, when they do and then encounter obstacles that we hadn't anticipated. A great deal of discernment is necessary to understand when we can help another person, when we need to let them find their own way through the difficulty they are facing, and when we need to encourage them to get professional counseling. Even when we are led by the Holy Spirit, there are areas that are best handled by those who have been specifically trained.

But lest you get discouraged, let me tell you that there is no greater joy than watching a person develop spiritually, emotionally, and relationally because he or she has adopted some of the principles and practices that you have found to be effective in your own life. In many ways the real test of a teacher and the real reward of a teacher are found in the one-on-one relationship.

In interviewing master teachers, I became even more aware of the importance of mentoring as I realized that many of the most effective teachers I know were themselves mentored by others. Sometimes it

Sometimes it takes a one-on-one relationship to bring out in any of us the best of our God-given talents.

takes a one-on-one relationship to bring out in any of us the best of our God-given talents. To encourage you in the worthwhile work of conducting a classroom of one, I share here some of the experiences of master teachers and their early mentors. In Ron Mahurin's case, it was a matter of being placed with those who knew more than he did and who were willing to share what they knew with a fledging teacher:

One of the early experiences I had as a new faculty member at Westmont College was to team-teach a course with colleagues from history and philosophy. Both colleagues were more senior than I and both had received awards from the college for their outstanding teaching. Being in the classroom with good teachers, and spending time outside of the classroom together discussing our subject matter, the students, and the approaches we wanted to take in introducing our students to the topics all stimulated my understanding of pedagogy.

One scholar (who prefers to remain unnamed) connected one-on-one with a Bible teacher who saw his ability and his desire to learn and grow and, as a result of those observations, was willing to spend time mentoring, guiding, and even criticizing to enable this future Bible teacher to develop that gift that was within him.

I was studying mathematics at Cambridge University and had a Bible teaching mentor. I heard him teach, then developed a friendship with him. He and I then taught together. He criticized me. It is crucial to learn to accept criticism in developing the gift of teaching. It is very, very important.

For Bill Rudd, several adults recognized in him a unique gift of communicating the message of the Bible and sought opportunities for him to exercise that gift even as a young teenager. Bill recounts that all of these experiences led him to a recognition of God's true calling on his life.

A series of people took me under their wings. First was a Youth for Christ director who gave me opportunities to speak at youth rallies and at little churches around the Upper Peninsula of Michigan. At about 13, I was asked by my pastor to teach kindergarten Sunday School. He also had me teach an InterVarsity group on a nearby college campus. At 13 or 14, I held weekend evangelistic meetings at another church. I also preached at the local rescue mission and on the street. During my sophomore year in college, I talked to my dad (who was a dentist) about the possibility of changing my major so that I could go into medicine. He agreed to support me whatever I decided to do, but he said, "Don't forget that God has given you a gift." I prayed about my decision. It was then that I knew that if I couldn't preach, I didn't want to live.

Kathleen Sindorf tells the story of how her experience in mentoring an intern wanting to learn about broadcasting opened her eyes to the joys of teaching and eventually led her to teaching broadcasting, media, and writing at three universities and teaching the Bible with Kay Arthur at Precept Ministries. Here is how a future master teacher began as a reluctant mentor and found unique satisfaction in a one-on-one teaching/learning relationship with a student:

When I began my college years, I took some education classes and went as far as a teaching practicum. At that point, I decided that classroom teaching was not for me. A few years later, when I was at CBN, the organization started a university (later to become Regent University). The school sent an intern to learn broadcasting by working with and observing me. I really didn't want an intern and didn't know what to do with her. She sat patiently watching me work. Then, one day, she sweetly asked, "Tell me what you're thinking about." That began a conversation which led to another and another. I found out how much fun it was to teach someone who really wanted to learn. We got to be such good friends through this process. Through her, I learned about how rewarding the collaborative creative process can be.

In our culture, numbers seem to be the measure of a teacher's success. But, God is the only one who can truly measure the effectiveness of what we do for him. Sometimes it is influencing only one life that will, in God's eyes, make our years of study and prayer worthwhile eternally. As we open ourselves to the possibility of building our experience and understanding into the lives of others, there are a few, but only a few, guidelines that will help us.

- Wait to be asked. Those of us who teach sometimes are the proverbial "know-it-alls." We think we have the answers for everyone, and we are more than willing to let them know. In God's perfect plan, though, timing is more important than having the right answers. It is critical that God have an opportunity to prepare the heart of the person to be mentored so that he or she will be ready to be taught. A ready learner is a joy to teach.

Jesus himself is our example here. When he was leaving Jericho, blind Bartimaeus sat alongside the road and heard that Jesus was passing by. He began to shout, "Jesus, Son of David, have mercy on me!"

But that was not a specific enough request for Jesus, so he responded by asking, "What do you want me to do for you?"

Bartimaeus answered, "Rabbi, I want to see." Based on the faith that this specific request represented, Jesus restored his sight. There are numerous other examples in the Gospels when Jesus required that the person making a request of him be very specific in asking for his help. Until the mentee recognizes the need in his life and, further, realizes that he must have help in meeting that need, even the Mentor of the Year cannot help him.

So, the general rule is to wait until someone asks you to mentor her, as Darla asked me. By the time someone is humble enough to ask for help, he is desperate enough to respond to the teaching.

- Confirm with God. Ultimately, we are working for our Father in heaven. So, I make it a practice never to take on a new project without his direction. This is particularly true, I believe, in the area of mentoring. Sometimes when someone seeks our help, they are truly needy and our hearts connect with theirs. We find ourselves wanting to help. But, if we are not the right person for that particular inquirer, we could conceivably do harm instead of good. Or, at the very least, we could cause a great deal of frustration for both ourselves and our student.

God knows who to put together and when, so I always make sure he is the final arbiter before I enter into a mentoring relationship with anyone. Ideally, God's direction should be sensed and understood by both the teacher and the student. That way, when disagreements or discouragements come in the mentoring process (and they will!), both can go back to the original design by God in bringing them together and can rely in faith that, until he directs a change of course, they are in his will and experiencing ultimately the mentoring of the divine Teacher.

- Listen first. Again, we must guard against having all the answers to questions our mentee is not asking. In Darla's case, she shared that she needed help with just about all aspects of her life: marriage, children, spiritual growth, home management, health, and so on. Others may be asking for mentoring assistance only in their spiritual lives or personal development. So, we must find out what they are seeking from us by listening to their words and, with discernment provided by the Holy Spirit, listening between the lines to hear their true heart.

- Design a plan. Effective teaching, as we already know, must be planned. Simply getting together with your mentee to discuss life is not enough. It might be an enjoyable time, but I predict that you will not make significant progress until you create and follow a plan of action. Follow a curriculum. Sometimes that may be as simple as going through a book together. At other times, as I did with Darla, you may need to write a learning plan that the two of you will go through together session by session until all the critical areas of the path of growth are covered. Enlist the help of your mentee in designing the plan. As we progress through our mentoring programs, there will be areas that our students will not be comfortable with, but if they helped to make the plan, they will be more willing and able to go through the difficult areas because they will understand the big picture, including the ultimate goals.

In Appendix II you will find the plan that I wrote for Darla. Because this was a whole life plan and it was written with a woman/homemaker in mind, it includes the following sections:

Home
Decorating: Creating a warm and welcoming environment
Management: Overseeing the smooth operation of your household
Organization: Preparing in advance to avoid stresses
Food: Providing appetizing, nutritional sustenance for your family

Children
Training: Building in the tools for productive, meaningful lives
Interaction: Developing family relationships that endure
Provision: Meeting family members' needs

Husband
Respecting: Building on his best qualities
Communicating: Expressing yourself effectively
Serving: Being Jesus in day-to-day life

God
Devotion: Relating one-on-one
Church: Relating with others who believe
Reaching out: Helping others in Jesus's name

Body
Fitness: Building physical strength
Food: Eating for nutrition and health
Beauty: Promoting what God has given

Development
Assessment: Figuring out where you are
Training: Learning what you need to know
Experience: Growing through the world around you

Please know that I do not purport to be an expert in each of these areas. But you do not have to be an expert in order to mentor effectively. My mentee already told me that she thought I knew more about living a productive, relational life than she did. I simply had to tell her what worked for me, help her to assess her own situation, and guide her into truth as I understood it from God's Word. When I get into specialized areas such as nutrition or decorating, I defer to experts and, therefore, recommend engaging the services of a decorator or reading well regarded books on health and nutrition. A mentor is a guide and a model as well as a teacher. We cannot know everything, but, in the case of mentoring, we do know more than the one we are teaching.

I have included the detailed mentoring program in this book just to provide you with a sample of a plan that worked for us. Of course, segments of the plan would have to be rewritten to be applied to mentoring a man as this plan was designed for a woman. The beauty of the mentoring relationship is that each plan is custom designed for the mentee's needs. There is no one plan for everyone but, because my relationship with Darla covered such a wide variety of life skills and subjects, this plan might be one you could borrow from and then redesign as needed.

- Work the plan. Darla and I found it very easy to get sidetracked in discussion about problems that came up in her life that sometimes discouraged her. Each time we got together, I devoted some time to dealing with these specifics, but I also tried to make sure that, before we left our session together, we returned to the learning plan in order to insure we made progress in the program we had developed. That way, there was a balance between the immediate problems to be addressed and the long-term goals of growth and learning to which we were committed. As we worked through these units together, Darla found that she was stronger in some areas than in others. So, some we went through fairly quickly, and others required more time, attention, and practice. In each unit, I provided for her a list of books and resources that she could turn to if she needed further help or simply wanted to dig a little deeper.

- Include God. Most of the time, Darla and I met in my study where there are two big leather chairs and an atmosphere of quiet and trust. We could talk freely and could go through our study materials together, but we also had complete freedom to spend time in prayer together before we parted. My advice to Darla without God's direction was empty and meaningless.

When we prayed together, we bonded to each other and to God and we committed our ways to him for direction and help. He never let us down!

Many of us have been mentored by others and we acknowledge that, without their input, their prayers, and their commitment of time to us, we would not be where we are today. At one point in my life I found myself as a single mother with two teen-aged daughters. I was at a loss many times in how to deal with the various issues that arose in our home. But I knew of a woman a few years older than I who had successfully raised four children of her own and who, with her husband, had taken in to their home nearly a hundred adolescents who had gone through the court system and needed help in getting their lives back in order. I never formally asked her to mentor me, but I did find myself scheduling lunch meetings with her every couple of months. We would talk about my daughters, how I was handling things, decisions that needed to be made, crises that were being faced, and so on. She talked from her experience, shared her wisdom, and prayed for me a lot. My girls are wonderful women of God today and much of the credit for their spiritual and emotional well-being goes to this dear woman who shared gently and confidently with me from her own experience.

Another time, I was working on my own spiritual walk and God brought Marge Lembke into my life, a woman who was further down the road than I was in terms of an intimate relationship with him. In this case, I did ask her to teach me, and she did. We have become great friends and partners in various ministry opportunities that God opens up, but our relationship still focuses around what we learn together in our approach to God, in our life of prayer and meditation, and in intercession for those God puts in our paths. The teaching she has provided has been intentional and effective partly because she is a godly woman and partly because God had prepared my heart to be a willing student eager to drink in her experience, her example, and her teaching.

If our teaching does not work on a one-on-one level, it does not work at all. Some who have a great teaching gift never stand in front of large crowds. Instead they find themselves with one student, one child, or one struggling saint and they minister one at a time to those who need instruction, guidance, and a life of example.

Jesus did both. He sometimes taught crowds of thousands and, at other times, we find him in deep conversation with a fallen Samaritan woman who was alone because no one else would be in her company, or with Nicodemus who came to see Jesus alone at night so that he could ask in private the gnawing questions of his heart. What results did Jesus have from this one-on-one teaching? The Samaritan woman excitedly went back and told her entire village about the one who told her everything she had ever done. Her changed life was more effective in reaching her neighbors than any evangelistic meetings that would have been held by the disciples! Nicodemus became one of the few religious leaders who acknowledged the true Messianic identity of Jesus and publicly showed his belief in Jesus by helping Joseph of Arimathea remove Jesus's body from the cross after he died.

Jesus shows us graphically the significance of one-at-a-time involvement with people who can benefit from our teaching. What about us?

 ## Let's Review and Evaluate

Are we willing to spend the one-on-one time with a person in need even though it is a ministry that takes us out of the spotlight?

Are we open to the specific feedback that we will receive from an individual who may not always agree with our prescription for his or her spiritual and personal growth?

Are we making ourselves available to the neediest among us?

Are we willing to seek the help of someone wiser and more experienced than we if there is an area in our lives where we need to be mentored?

EIGHT

TEN WARNINGS FOR TEACHERS

From all my lame defeats and oh! much more
From all the victories that I seemed to score;
From cleverness shot forth on Thy behalf
At which, while angels weep, the audience laugh;
From all my proofs of Thy divinity
Thou, who wouldst give no sign, deliver me.

—C. S. Lewis in *Poems*

This chapter will tell you a few things to beware of as you progress in your growth as a teacher of the Bible. You will learn that:

- You can handle criticism in positive ways.
- You can avoid being driven by perfectionism.
- Boldness in teaching may mean risk taking and may mean stress.
- Pride avoidance is a constant focus.
- The rewards of teaching *far* outweigh the difficulties faced.

I spoke to a friend of mine about the subject of this chapter. Barbara looked at me quizzically and wondered aloud what teachers needed to be "warned" about. A little later in our conversation, she told me about taking on a project in her church, teaching seven- and eight-year-old girls from disadvantaged families. On the way home after one of these meetings one evening, one of the other leaders turned to Barbara and began to compliment her on her ability to reach these little ones so effectively. As the praise went on, Barbara felt herself kind of liking what she was hearing. Maybe she did, in fact, have some special talents. Maybe she was able to connect with these children better than anyone else could. Maybe … . Later she realized that there was a little bit of pride growing where total humility used to be. As she recounted the incident, she suddenly brightened and said, "Now I know what you mean about warnings for teachers!"

As teachers, we are put in places of honor, we are considered authorities, and we are particularly prone to a bit of prideful arrogance. We talked about that in an earlier chapter, but there are several other warnings I think it important to mention, too. When we take on the responsibilities of teaching, there are a few things we should anticipate and, maybe even, be wary of. The better prepared for the kind of life we are called to, the less likely we are to be discouraged when some of these things happen to us. Preparedness is the key to keeping on. Let's take a look at ten of the issues to watch for as we engage in the teaching of God's Word.

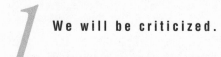

We will be criticized.

Teachers must be pretty tough. Not everyone will like what we have to say, and their disagreement with us may have nothing to do with the quality of our teaching, with our delivery style, with the way we look, or with our personalities. If we are willing to teach truth, and if we are willing to be conveyers of messages from God, sometimes our messages will be unpopular. It is normal, though, to want people to like us, and criticism can be hurtful.

When we are criticized, we should first ask ourselves honestly if the criticism is justified. Sometimes our attitude, our sensitivity, or our approach may need to be corrected. As Ravi Zacharias says,

Teaching the Bible and hammering the Bible on people's heads are two different things. If Jesus Christ is presented in his attractiveness, people are drawn to him. Hammering home pet peeves on particulars doesn't always succeed because it deals with issues rather than the worldview that generates the issues. So worldview and understanding are key if the Bible is to have maximum effect.

Tamara Rosier echoes a similar thought when she says,

Don't use the Bible as a weapon. As teachers, we need to meet the hurting person instead of giving them the definitive answer. Even if you know the answer they need, wait for the key moment when the person is ready to receive it.

And sometimes we are simply wrong. Sometimes we make mistakes and, when we do, we must be both confident enough and humble enough to correct those errors. Our goal, as teachers, is to convey truth. If we, in our humanness, have made a mistake in interpretation or presentation, then we must acknowledge our fault and correct it. I can remember agonizing each time prior to a "confession" of error on my part. In every case, however, the students have been overwhelmingly supportive and, I think, even liked knowing that I didn't believe I was perfect and that I could admit and correct my error.

> *Sometimes we make mistakes and, when we do, we must be both confident enough and humble enough to correct those errors.*

If, on the other hand the criticism is wrong and troubles us or becomes divisive, I suggest that we put the instruction of Matthew 18 into play and go to the critic for a one-on-one meeting. It is better to try to deal with such issues in private settings in order to avoid creating chaos and dissent in the classroom. If you and your critic cannot agree, you may agree to disagree. In so doing, you have allowed your critic to maintain his dignity and you have preserved unity in your teaching setting. Proving yourself right to another is not as important as being true to God's Word and the message he has given you to present.

If it is any consolation (and, to me, it is), Jesus was criticized more than you or I will ever be. Of course, he never had to acknowledge a mistake and, in his case, he took on his critics in public arenas. That is because he was God, was perfect, always had the appropriate attitude, and always had the right answer. I am not so fortunate, nor are you! But I do point this out just to acknowledge that there may be times when a critic needs to be addressed publicly. When that is the case, we must do so with much spiritual and academic preparation. And, always, always, always, we must do so in love. Our students will respect us if we don't lose our cool, but respond with kindness.

Jesus, as always, is our best example here. Look at what he says in Luke 13:34, "O Jerusalem, Jerusalem, you who kill the prophets and stone those sent to you, how often I have longed to gather your children together, as a hen gathers her chicks under her wings, but you were not willing!" The religious leaders in Jerusalem were noted for their intolerance of prophets and teachers sent to them to deliver God's message. They not only criticized them, they killed them. They were serious about their opposition to those who didn't follow the party line! Now Jesus, who is on his way to Jerusalem when he says these words, knows that they have rejected his message and will kill him, too. I am sure he didn't like being criticized or rejected any more than we do, but look at his heart. After he reminds them of their hatred toward the truth of God and his messengers, he reveals his heart of love for these rebellious and stubborn people. He just wants to hold them close, but they resist. They are more interested in being right in their own eyes than in having a relationship with their Savior. But his love never wavers even when it seems there is nothing in them to love. Do we have any critics like that?

Warren Wiersbe gives a great concluding thought on these matters:

Not everybody agrees on the interpretation of the Bible, but St. Augustine said it well, "In essentials, unity; in non-essentials, liberty; in all things, charity."

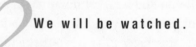

We will be watched.

Teaching is a very public activity. When I taught high school, I considered myself privileged to live about forty miles away from my school. That way, when I went to the grocery store, I didn't run into my students and have to act like their teacher. That is no longer the case for me. My students are right here in my backyard (some literally!), down the street, and in most of the stores and restaurants I frequent. If my behavior in the public arena is not consistent with my teaching in the classroom, my credibility is lost.

Now, I have a choice. I can choose to pretend to be something I am not and, that way, be on edge every time I walk outside my door, or I can be real. If I am an authentic teacher, living out what I am teaching should become more and more natural. I am not perfect, though, and will not live my faith and my teaching perfectly. In spite of my shortcomings, God keeps on working with me and is teaching me as I teach others that I am in process. So I have to be real, acknowledge areas of need, recognize areas of weakness, and be honest with my students. For the most part, students will accept such honesty and then give me some latitude if they see me doing something they think is not consistent with my teaching. Hopefully, if I have been suitably vulnerable with them, they will feel free to approach me (at an appropriate time, of course) if they are uncomfortable with some characteristic that they saw in me.

Here's the burden that is placed upon us as teachers: "A student is not above his teacher, but everyone who is fully trained will be like his teacher" (Luke 6:40). This is a double warning to us: First we must be careful who we learn from because we will become like those whose teaching we follow. Second, we have to be authentic in our walk with God. Others are watching and will emulate us. That is why Paul says to his protégé, Timothy, "… set an example for the believers in speech, in life, in love, in faith, and in purity" (I Timothy 4:12b).

3 We are never done studying.

When we teach the Bible, we are handling a very powerful thing given by a God whose desire was to communicate to humankind who he is, how much he cares, and the means he has provided to reconcile us to himself. That is a very important message and, as teachers, we must not get it wrong. We must study God's Word, meditate on it, and allow the Holy Spirit to teach us. Only then will we be equipped to teach others. As one master teacher says, "Get into Scripture and get to know God." Sounds to me like an assignment that can never be completed! So we keep at it throughout our lives.

Again, Paul, writing to Timothy says, "Watch your life and doctrine closely. Persevere in them, because if you do, you will save both yourself and your hearers." (I Timothy 4:16) and, again in his next letter, "Do your best to present yourself to God as one approved, a workman who does not need to be ashamed and who correctly handles the word of truth" (II Timothy 2:15). Both directives indicate a necessity for study, for certainty in the accuracy of what we are teaching, and for careful diligence in our preparation. We are not teaching history or English or mathematics. We are teaching the very message of God. We can never be worthy messengers, but we must take the responsibility very seriously.

When we prepare a message or a lesson, if we are in doubt about any point of doctrine, we should either wait before we deliver that part of the lesson, or be honest with our students, letting them know that we have not been able to come to a final conclusion on our interpretation of a certain verse or teaching. Most students would rather have us be honest about what we are not sure of than to be dogmatic when we should not be. You may have heard the story about the pastor who had penciled in the margin of his sermon notes, "Weak point. Shout!" It may have worked for him, but it's bad advice generally. If we have a weak point, we should either make it stronger by appropriate study, or present it in humility and with caution.

Many of us are teaching the Bible without any formal seminary training. I am in that category, too. I have had a little bit of Greek study, but am not even close to being an expert. How can I teach the Bible with confidence if I don't know the original languages? I admit my deficiency and rely on others who are experts. Dr. Rex Rogers says that reading on a broad range of subjects sharpens his thinking and prepares him for teaching:

I find that if I am at a period in my life when I cannot read a lot, it affects my vocabulary and ability to deliver in the classroom. Reading shapes my mind; ideas flow when I read a lot and on a wide variety of subjects.

We have the advantage, these days, of easy access to the best in scholarship and information. A well stocked bookshelf is a help, as is the Internet, and Bible study software. We will give more details on these resources in the next chapter.

But the primary caution here is to make sure that we, to the extent possible, understand the message that God intended in Scripture and that we never, never, never use Scripture to support our own message. Other master teachers warn us in this regard:

Don't use what I call "Godspeak." There are those who are always saying, "I feel the Lord is telling me this." Often statements like that can be manipulative and can be used to promote guilt in others. God does direct us, but I caution teachers and leaders to be very careful in attributing particular words or instructions as being from God unless they are in the written text of God's Word.

—Dr. Tamara Rosier

Don't get in the way of the text. It is a temptation to teachers to draw attention to ourselves instead of to the Lord. It is also easy for us to read our own agendas into the text instead of listening to the text and following its voice.

—Dr. Don Denyes

We teach to express and not to impress. A true Bible teacher is a servant and not a celebrity—or a guru. The most important part of our life is the part that only God sees, so we must be "abiding" in Christ. Without Him, we can do nothing.

—Dr. Warren Wiersbe

The message is God's, and it is our awe-inspiring responsibility to communicate it as he intended. To do less or more is to adulterate his Word, and we will be held accountable. God has given us a tremendous trust.

4 We will be driven.

For those of us who have taught for awhile, we can identify with Peter and John when they said, "For we cannot help speaking about what we have seen and heard" (Acts 4:20). One of the dangers of teaching is that it can be all-consuming. We learn because we love to learn. But, like sponges, we soak up so much information that we have to leak it out. Thus, teaching is born in us! If you are like me, the passion just grows. The more I learn, the more I want to learn. The more I take in, the greater the desire to give out.

If I am not sensitive to the leading of the Spirit in my life, who sometimes slows me down, I will be driven. God wants us to learn and to teach, but he does not want us to be controlled by anything or anyone other than the Holy Spirit. So, there are times where we all need to take a break from teaching and from study. In my case, my class will run for a ten- or twelve-week session, then we take a few weeks off before we begin again. Those few weeks breathe freshness into me, into my study, and into my teaching. I get renewed and energized.

At other times, renewal may come from going to lunch with a friend, giving a good day's work to our employers, washing the car, getting groceries, or walking to the mailbox. We must resist the temptation to be so immersed in our study and our teaching that we do not become fully developed persons.

We should be well rounded in our relationships, to be sure, but also in our study. If we have ongoing teaching responsibilities, it is natural for us to focus the main body of our reading and study around the subject we are teaching. Many of the experts interviewed for this book recommended a broad reading list for those of us who teach. We can learn much from reading classic literature, for example, as it deals with universal and timeless themes that are often applicable to our teaching. We also should be aware of current events and trends in our world today so that we can be conversant with our friends and students and also so that we can guide our students as they process what they see and hear in the world. If our teaching does not touch the real lives of our students, it will not be effective in the long run.

5 We will be stressed.

Teaching can hurt. We take personal risk when we begin to love our students, when we begin to get involved in their lives, and when we agonize over their personal and spiritual growth. No one knew this better than the Apostle Paul. In his second letter to the Corinthians, he recounted all the times he had been beaten, stoned, shipwrecked, and all the other discomforts he suffered as he traveled throughout Asia Minor presenting the message of Christ. At the end of that long list of horrible physical sufferings, he says, "And that's not the half of it, when you throw in the daily pressures and anxieties of all the churches. When someone gets to the end of his rope, I feel the desperation in my bones. When someone is duped into sin, an angry fire burns in my gut" (II Corinthians 11:28–29, *The Message*). If I read this literally, he is saying that the personal involvement with the churches was more stressful to him than the physical torments he endured. Look at the words he chooses: pressures, anxieties, desperation, anger. These are stress words, to be sure! And the stress that he feels has grown directly out of his teaching and his personal involvement with his students.

Are we ready for that? Running a business or managing a zoo would be less stressful! When we choose to accept God's invitation to teach his Word to his children, we enter a very emotional world. There are many people we will grow to love who will fall away from the truth they have learned from us. And it hurts. There are others who will go through great personal trauma. And we feel their pain. There are those who say they understand what we teach, but we see no change in their lives. And we ache for them. As teachers, we put our hearts on the line. We put all our energies, emotions, intellect, and spirituality into what we teach. We begin to love our students as Jesus loves us. And, in doing so, we become vulnerable to being hurt.

We also make ourselves accessible. That means, there may be late night phone calls from students in crisis. Or counseling those (usually at inconvenient times) who are in long-term stress situations relating, often, to health, wayward children, or marriages. We listen, we pray with them, and we move on. But their burdens become our burdens (a la Galatians 6:2) and we soon discover that, by putting God's gift of teaching into practice, we have taken upon ourselves many burdens. If we learn to turn those burdens over to our Lord by praying them to him, we will not become overburdened by the troubles and stresses of others. But there are times when we feel the weight of the cares and responsibilities of teaching.

6 We will take risks.

Have you ever spoken out in a conversation, then played back in your mind what you just said, and asked yourself, "*Where* did *that* come from?" If what you said was scripturally sound, if it related accurately to the topic at hand, and if it was delivered with conviction and love, you may have just been a "conduit" of the Holy Spirit's boldness!

Here's what the apostles prayed, "Now, Lord, consider their threats and enable your servants to speak your word with great boldness" (Acts

4:29). What happens next is pretty exciting. "After they prayed, the place where they were meeting was shaken. And they were all filled with the Holy Spirit and spoke the word of God boldly" (Acts 4:31). If we are submitting ourselves to the leading of the Spirit and allowing him to guide our study and our teaching, we will find ourselves in places where boldness is required. If speaking out is what God wants us to do, he will give us the confidence and the ready response. And we may shake our heads and wonder how *those* words ever came out of *our* mouths. Many of us who are teachers are quiet and somewhat reclusive by nature. Bold is not exactly what we want to be. But, if God has a message for us to give, boldness may be required—and he is willing to deliver the boldness to us so that we can deliver his message to others.

Part of the reason we prefer reticence to boldness is that delivering God's message may not put us on a "most popular people" list. In fact, we may make some people mad. That was certainly true in Stephen's case. In Chapter 6 of Acts, we see him in debate with some of the Jewish religious leaders and we read, "These men began to argue with Stephen, but they could not stand up against his wisdom or the Spirit by whom he spoke" (Acts 6:10). Stephen was certainly made bold by the Spirit and that boldness resulted in a confrontation. The confrontation made his listeners so angry that they actually stoned Stephen to death, a biblical warning that not everyone will like what we have to say or the boldness with which we say it!

Many times our message will be accepted, acknowledged, and, if we are fortunate, made a part of the lives of our listeners. But when the message we are called to share is of the sometimes difficult and harsh truth of God, we must proclaim it boldly. We don't look for conflict, but we must show courage when God sends us to the front lines.

We will give up our independence.

George Muller, who lived in England during the 1800s, is probably best known for the establishment of orphanages in that country and for the life of faith he lived. Although Muller never asked for monetary support for the children he housed and cared for, people donated more than $7 million to support the orphans. His reliance on the Holy Spirit for provision was amazing. But many do not know that he learned at one point in his life to rely on the Holy Spirit for teaching, as well.

Early in his life, having experienced health problems in London, he was advised to retreat for some time to the country in order to breathe fresh air and recover from his illness. His physical retreat became a spiritual retreat as well. James Lawson, in his book *Deeper Experiences of Famous Christians,* recounts Muller's own words about it: "The result was that *the first evening that I shut myself into my room to give myself to prayer and meditation over the Scriptures, I learned more in a few hours than I had done during a period of several months previously* ... In addition to these truths, it pleased the Lord to lead me to see a higher standard of devotedness than I had seen before" (page 245, italics added). As he read his Bible over the next days, the Spirit enlightened his mind and taught him truths he had not understood before. He returned to London refreshed in body and, more so, refreshed in spirit and mind.

Have you ever felt that you study and study and the learning comes so slowly? Or as much as you read and dig into Scripture, you cannot come up with just the right text or just the right teaching for the lesson you are preparing? The Muller story caught my attention because he was able to condense hours and hours of study into just a short time. With the Holy Spirit's help and direction, clarity and understanding came much more quickly. When I am under time pressure, this seems like a very good plan! I also know that, without the Holy Spirit's help, I can spend hours and hours and not come up with anything of substance to share with my class. Consciously yielding my time, my thoughts, and my preparation to him is essential for finding and sharing the message that he has for my students.

By the way, when Muller returned to London, he couldn't wait to tell others what he had learned and, a short time thereafter in an effort to share those truths, became the pastor of a little church in Devonshire and also began to preach in surrounding towns. Once he had been taught by the Spirit, he had much to share with others and he pastored various churches during his life. Then, following an even greater calling later in his life, from the time he was seventy until the age of ninety he traveled more than 200,000 miles around the world preaching to thousands—no small feat in the late 1800s! *(Deeper Experiences of Famous Christians,* pp. 236–249).

George Muller is a great example of what can happen in the life of a man or woman who gives up control to God. Bible teachers are sent to present the messages that God gives us to share. As a result, we find that we are no longer independent agents choosing to teach what we like and ignoring subjects that are not as interesting to us or as fun to teach. Instead, we willingly subject ourselves to the leadership of the Holy Spirit. When we do, amazing things happen.

First of all, we will be teaching what God wants us to teach. He knows our students and their immediate needs. He knows what they are ready to hear and what will be most effective in their lives at the moment. So, having his direction in choice of topic and emphasis is of great significance.

Second, because God wrote the book, he can help us understand it so that we can teach it with authority. Remember the reaction to Jesus's teaching? His hearers stated that " … he taught as one who had authority, and not as their teachers of the law" (Matthew 7:29). They could tell that he knew what he was talking about! The teachers of the law, though, were no slouches. They studied hard (probably a lot harder than you and I do), they knew their material, and they probably had worked out all the best presentation methods. But they didn't have the one key ingredient that Jesus had: authority.

Consider Matthew 28:18–20, in which Jesus is giving some final instructions to his disciples before he leaves the earth, "All authority in heaven and earth has been given to me. Therefore, go and make disciples of all nations, baptizing them in the name of the Father and of the Son and of the Holy Spirit, and teaching them to obey everything I have commanded you … " Did you notice that Jesus precedes this command to teach with a statement about his authority? Why did he do that? I think it is because he was passing that authority on to his disciples whom he was now sending to teach others. He wanted them to teach with the same authority he had. Their listeners would know the difference.

We don't want to be like the biblical teachers of the law who knew their material well, but taught without ringing conviction. Instead, Jesus has given his own authority to those he has sent to make disciples and to teach. We access that authority by giving up our independence and declaring our total dependence on the guidance and enlightenment of the Holy Spirit.

8 We will be stalked by pride.

As the C. S. Lewis quote at the beginning of this chapter humorously reminds us, and as we mentioned briefly earlier, pride is a great risk for those who teach the truths of God. We find just the right turn of phrase, we have some great spiritual insight, we make an argument that no one can counter, or we discover and present a brand new scriptural truth. We must be pretty intelligent. More intelligent than most. Our students should be pretty grateful to have our brain power working for them. See what I mean? We need to constantly remind ourselves that we have nothing that God did not give us. The message is his, the book we teach is his, the students come because he sends them to us, and our ability to read and comprehend is a gift with which he has entrusted us. It is nothing from us and everything from him.

When I talked to master teachers about warnings they would pass on to those of us who are teaching the Bible, the overwhelming single warning related to pride. Here are a few quotes from those who have faced the monster of pride:

Keep going back to God. Don't start to feel that teaching is about you, you, you. All I have in terms of ideas and abilities have been given to me by God. I start to lose the creative edge I have and become inhibited if I begin to get arrogant or proud.

—Nataly Berckmann

Beware of what I call "Theological Snobbery." It is an attitude stemming from education that often communicates that only a certain few have the training to teach or to know truth. They throw around terms like "unbiblical" and convey an arrogant, self-righteous pride in their education and knowledge. My friend, you can learn from anyone. Jesus's disciples in Acts were noted as unlearned and unlettered, but they had been with Jesus. The great commission suggests that what we teach others is what Jesus is teaching us. This is not a disdain for education, but a warning of its ability to puff you up.

—Rev. William Dondit

We have to be careful not to get into the "me" mode. It is easy to think it is all about us when people are giving more credit than we deserve and we are liking it. If we are not careful, our success can lead to our desire and ability to manipulate the crowd.

Instead, we need to be as objective and open as possible about the Scripture and let it lead what we teach.

—Dr. Don Denyes

As a teacher of the Bible, it is very easy to get spiritually arrogant. You know so much and you study the Bible extensively while others don't even have regular devotions. Teaching the Bible requires humility. You have to be willing to share your struggles and your failures. It is so easy to think that you must be great since everyone is looking to you for teaching.

—Kathleen O. Sindorf

A humble and teachable spirit is very important. We minister sometimes to people who are more expert on the anecdotal material or even the theme we are dealing with. A haughty spirit is a huge barrier to effective teaching and example.

—Dr. Ravi Zacharias

Watch your ego. God will honor true humility of spirit and an openness and acknowledgment of our own weakness and frailty.

—Dr. Ron Mahurin

One way to ensure that we will not become arrogant or conceited about any teaching success that we have is to make sure that all the glory goes to God. Sounds trite, doesn't it? But we know that, biblically, it is sound advice. So how do we do it? When someone gives us a compliment, we are to accept it graciously. To respond by putting ourselves down or by denying the power of the teaching is to tell the person giving the compliment that they don't know what they're talking about. That is argumentative and unkind. It is better to accept the praise with a simple "Thank you" or with a question, "What was most helpful to you in the teaching?" Then, just as soon as we are alone with God (maybe in the car on the way home), we give to him the praise that we just received. We simply pray it back to him. We tell him how powerful the teaching was and thank him for making it so. Verbally and from our hearts we give him honor and glory and praise for speaking to our classes from his Word. That way, praise will not become a danger to us. We will simply receive it temporarily and then offer it with thanksgiving to the one we serve. We don't make it our own.

One of my favorite stories about pride avoidance comes from Mother Theresa. It is said that a reporter came to her after she was awarded the Nobel Peace Prize. He asked her if she, who was the very epitome of humility, was worried that all the public acclaim she was receiving would go to her head and she would become proud. In her own recognizable fashion, Mother Theresa paused for a moment and then said, "Do you remember the time that Jesus rode into Jerusalem on the back of a donkey and all the people were shouting 'hosanna" and waving palm branches, and throwing their clothes down to make a path?"

"Yes, I do," the reporter answered.

"Do you think the donkey thought it was for him?"

A zinger, to be sure! We are but donkeys who carry the Christ. All eyes should be on him, not us. If we do it right, that's what will happen and we will be protected from the ugly morass of pride.

9 We will be tempted.

We all are aware of the shame brought on the name of Jesus by the public falls of nationally known television evangelists a few years ago. One was involved in sexual sin with a prostitute and another was involved in dishonesty in dealing with large amounts of money sent in by his listening audience. Both men were well known and highly regarded by millions of people who watched their broadcasts faithfully, and they were thought to be men of God who were honestly and conscientiously teaching God's Word. I believe they started out that way. When they first opened the Bible and began to teach, they never intended to bilk anyone out of thousands of dollars and they certainly never intended to lead sexually immoral lives. But what happened?

I believe it is as if those who are in the public eye, whether it is the eye of a national audience or a Sunday School class, have imaginary targets painted on them so that Satan will know right where to throw his flaming arrows (Ephesians 6:16). The evil one does not want the Word of God to be taught. He often thinks that if he can disable the teacher, he will disable the message. Sometimes he is successful. The Ephesians 6 passage referenced previously gives us the "armor" we need to counteract Satan's attacks. Our arsenal includes truth, righteousness, the message of the gospel, faith, salvation, the Word of God, and prayer. We are told that, with these weapons, to "take your stand against the devil's schemes" (Ephesians 6:11b).

Now, if an enemy is going to attack us, he will not randomly shoot arrows and hope to hit the target. We can bet that the target Satan has on us is affixed firmly to our weakest point. One way to effectively shield ourselves from his attacks and temptations is to take some time to assess where our vulnerabilities lie. Is it in gaining approval from others? Does it relate to our sexuality? Is it in desire for material things? Is it living in anxiety or worry? Is it being susceptible to pride? Or treating others with arrogance? Is it impatience? Or lack of love? Once we have identified our areas of weakness, we can be alert and aware of our vulnerabilities. Then, we need to take those areas to God in prayer and ask that he strengthen us where we are weak. Over time, as we submit to his authority in our lives, we will become stronger.

But we never will be beyond temptation in this life. Jesus, the perfect man, was tempted over and over again during his lifetime. His mission was so great and so important that Satan was not about to let up on his efforts to deter Jesus from fulfilling what God had sent him to do. Those with a calling to teach are also on a mission, and there is an enemy who does not want to see that mission fulfilled. Peter states this pretty clearly when he warned, "Be self-controlled and alert. Your enemy the devil prowls around like a roaring lion looking for someone to devour" (I Peter 5:8). He goes on to advise that we are to resist him by standing firm in the faith. We must not be surprised by temptation nor discouraged by it. Satan does not bother to tempt those who are not a threat to him. We know that, with the power of God, we can stand up to any temptation the evil one sends our way. We do not need to give in to the pull to do wrong, but, by definition, temptation is tempting. It is difficult to overcome, but every time we say "no" to it, we grow in our faith and God rewards our commitment to do the right thing even when it is the hard thing.

10

We will be held accountable.

In the first three chapters of his first letter to the Corinthians, Paul carefully explains that he did not come to them with worldly wisdom, impressive rhetoric, or well orchestrated orations. Instead, he just talked to them about Christ, about the cross, and about the access they have to God through Jesus. Then he begins Chapter 4 with these words, "Don't imagine us leaders to be something we aren't. We are servants of Christ, not his masters. We are guides into God's most sublime secrets, not security guards posted to protect them. The requirements for a good guide are reliability and accurate knowledge. It matters very little to me what you think of me, even less where I rank in popular opinion. I don't even rank myself. Comparisons in these matters are pointless. I'm not aware of anything that would disqualify me from being a good guide for you, but that doesn't mean much. The Master makes that judgment" (I Corinthians 4:1–4 *The Message.*)

There are a couple of things to notice in this text. First, we are "guides into God's most sublime secrets." If that doesn't make us shiver with the excitement of what we teach, nothing will. A great trust. A great responsibility.

Second, there is only one person we have to please in our teaching: Jesus. Paul makes it clear that he didn't care how popular he was with his audience. His only concern was with how the Master would judge him. Jesus is the ultimate judge of whether we are good teachers, whether we have been faithful to the text, whether we have loved our students, and whether our lives have been consistent with the truths we teach. He knows us inside and out. We cannot hide from him our motives, our secret faults, or our insecurities. We must make it our goal to be honest with him always, to pray constantly, and to present his Word as truthfully, and as humbly as we are able. Then, some day, we will hear Jesus say, "Well done, good and faithful servant! ... Come and share your master's happiness!" (Matthew 25:23). Now, won't that be a great day?

Let's Review and Evaluate

How are we doing in these areas?

Do any of the ten warnings in this chapter strike your mind as being of particular importance to you? Go to God with your concerns and allow him to direct your thoughts and your protection.

Are we regularly practicing spiritual disciplines so that we are strengthened internally against temptation and growing in our knowledge of the God we serve?

Are we committed to teaching God's truth even after we realize the possible pain and difficulties that such a commitment may bring?

We should not take these warnings as reasons to be frightened, but, instead, should allow them to help us see the importance of the calling that we have. Teaching God's truths is a job not to be taken lightly. It is one with great rewards (we'll take a look at those later) both in this life and for eternity, but with those great rewards also come great responsibility and risk. We are not in this alone. The Holy Spirit is our teacher, our comforter, our helper, and our guide. When our faithfulness is combined with the Spirit's resources, we are able to present God's word with boldness, effectiveness, and great joy!

NINE

RESOURCES FOR TEACHERS

Getting the facts is only half the job;
the other half is to use them intelligently.

—E. C. McKenzie in *14,000 Quips and Quotes*

This chapter will help you in these areas:

- Building a library of basic Bible study books.
- Learning to find valuable resources on the Internet and via computer software.
- Gleaning from others in areas of public speaking and skill development.
- Finding stories, illustrations, and real-life examples.
- Reading on a broad range of topics.

This chapter will direct you to resources to help you prepare, present, and improve the material that you teach. The resources I mention here are those that I have found helpful. As you progress in your study and in your teaching, you will find others that speak particularly to your learning style or to the topics that you teach. I have experienced great enjoyment as I build a library of resources to have at my fingertips as I study and prepare lessons, and I hope you will, too. This chapter offers guidance on where to begin in this process. Here are some of my favorite resources:

Following the Holy Spirit

We have talked about this throughout this book, but I must reiterate here that the first and primary resource for any teacher of the Bible is the Spirit of God himself. Jesus told his disciples, "When he, the Spirit of truth, comes, he will guide you into all truth … He will bring glory to me by taking from what is mine and making it known to you" (John 16:13a and 14). Paul described God's Word as truth (II Timothy 2:15). So, the Holy Spirit guides us to a more complete, more accurate understanding of the Bible. As Bible teachers, we dare not approach God's Word without the enlightenment of God's Spirit.

Additionally, we are told that the Holy Spirit gives us power. When Jesus was about to leave this earth, he told his followers, "But you will receive power when the Holy Spirit comes on you; and you will be my witnesses in Jerusalem, and in all Judea and Samaria, and to the ends of the earth" (Acts 1:8). They were not to begin their preaching and teaching until the Spirit came to empower them. You and I can teach with all our might, but we will never accomplish anything of benefit in the Kingdom of God until we allow the Spirit to control and empower us.

The following are brief descriptions of books that have been helpful to me as I have developed my dependence on the leading of the Holy Spirit. For me, they inspired the notion that God does, in fact, relate to me in the events of my daily life, he does have a plan for my serving him, and he will reveal that plan if I am willing to listen and respond to his direction. I do not necessarily agree with everything written in each of these books. You, as a student of God's Word, must sort for yourselves what is in keeping with your understanding and what may be contrary to it. But, in general, these books opened my eyes to new and enlightening ways that the Spirit is at work in my life and in my teaching.

• *The Helper*

This book, by Catherine Marshall, tells her own story of learning to walk in step with the leading of the Holy Spirit. As she relates her own experiences, she uses the book as an opportunity to provide scriptural teaching about the work and various roles of the Spirit in our lives. I find myself revisiting it often.

• *Surprised by the Voice of God*

This book, by Jack Deere, was especially interesting to me because it was written by a seminary professor who, for most of his life, related to God on a pretty intellectual level. Then, he began to sense God speaking in specific ways in his life and, eventually, he began actively to seek those messages from the Holy Spirit. *Surprised by the Voice of God* is a scriptural defense and personal testimony of the practice of listening for, recognizing, and responding to the work and direction and affirmation of the Spirit in lives of Christians.

• *A Listening Ear*

This short book by physician Paul Tournier is a collection of talks he gave throughout his professional career. Of greatest interest to me were his personal accounts of listening for God to lead him, to fill his mind with the right thoughts, and to transform him into the person God wanted him to be. For many years of his life, he practiced waiting on God for one hour each morning, often with his wife at his side. He would write down whatever thoughts God placed into his mind during this time of meditative waiting. From that first hour, he lived his day. "I wait for God to stimulate my thoughts sufficiently to renew me, to make me creative instead of being what St. Paul calls a tinkling cymbal. It's the cornerstone of my life. It is an attempt at seeing people and their problems from God's point of view, insofar as that is possible." (pp. 12–13). The change that occurred in Tournier as a result of these listening times with God was so great that he was among the first to write books on medical practices that treat the whole person and not just the physical body.

• *The Heavenly Man*

Written by Brother Yun with Paul Hattaway, this is the true story of a Chinese Christian, Brother Yun, who was persecuted to the point of death many times for his faith, yet survived and persevered, always trusting God. The book is full of power-packed quotes from the mouth of this man, all of which inspire us as followers of Christ. His own conversion story is one of clear revelation by the Holy Spirit. His obedience to every direction of the Spirit led him to be a church leader in China even though his leadership was often exercised from a jail cell. Presently he lives in Europe and heads the Back to Jerusalem movement whereby Chinese Christians are committed to reaching out to the Muslim world until the Gospel message reaches from them westward to Jerusalem where the message began.

• *Amazing Faith*

This book by Michael Richardson is the authorized biography of Bill Bright, founder of Campus Crusade of Christ. Many times in Bill's life, he sensed the specific direction of the Holy Spirit in his teaching and in the establishment of this worldwide organization. "God in an unusual way opened my mind, touched my heart … I can't translate into English or any other language what happened, but God met with me." (p. 61). Bright actively sought the leadership of the Spirit and, in fact, engaged in seven 40-day fasts during his lifetime. The purpose of the fasts was not to get God to do something for him, but, instead, to seek God's face and direction. The ministry he established now has 27,000 full-time staff members and up to a half million trained volunteers who serve in 196 countries around the world.

• *Is That Really You, God?*

This is the autobiography of Loren Cunningham, founder of Youth with a Mission (YWAM). He tells amazing stories of being led by the Holy Spirit, of messages received which helped to direct the ministry and to teach those who would then teach others. The result of following the guidance of the Holy Spirit was the establishment of a strong helping ministry as well as many schools for theological study around the world. At the end of the book is a helpful section entitled "Hearing the Voice of God," in which, using much scriptural support, the author outlines twelve guides for tuning in to the Holy Spirit's leading.

• *God's Smuggler*

This classic book by Brother Andrew (with John and Elizabeth Sherrill) recounts story after story of the Spirit's leadership in the life of Brother Andrew as he began to bring Bibles into countries governed by those who were closed to its message. He brought them in the backs of cars and eventually in huge boatloads, always under cover, but also under the guidance and protection of the Holy Spirit. The stories are sometimes harrowing but give great testimony to the power of listening with obedient hearts to the voice of God through his Spirit in our lives.

• *Deeper Experiences of Famous Christians*
The author, James Gilchrist Lawson, has researched the lives of some of the best known Christians throughout history and tells how the Holy Spirit guided their lives and broadened and empowered their ministries. The biographical information is inspirational to aspiring teachers and pastors and includes the lives of the following: George Fox, John Bunyan, George Whitefield, Charles Finney, D. L. Moody, General Booth, and many others.

Finding the Right Story

A teacher is always on the hunt for illustrations, stories, humor, or the right turn of phrase. First, we know instinctively that parabolic truth surrounds us. We just have to be aware of situations that occur in our lives and how those experiences can be turned into illustrations of spiritual truths as we teach others. The only way I know to develop that awareness is to write things down. Many teachers recommend journaling as a way to record resource material. I have found, however, that I don't go back to read my journals often enough to glean material for teaching. Instead, I keep a file of notes of incidents in my life— everything from pumping gas at the self-serve station to conversations with my grandson to relationship lessons I learn from my cat. Almost everything that happens to us can have a spiritual application. We just have to develop the discipline to see our lives in a spiritual light.

Sometimes we need stories or quotations from others. You can buy books of stories that may be helpful. Some that I use are as follows:

Nelson's Complete Book of Stories, Illustrations & Quotes
(Robert J. Morgan)

14,000 Quips and Quotes
(E. C. McKenzie)

Phillips' Book of Great Thoughts and Funny Sayings
(Bob Phillips)

Great Thoughts, Revised and Updated
(George Seldes)

12,000 Inspirational Quotations
(Frank S. Mead)

The Quotable Lewis
(Wayne Martindale and Jerry Root)

The Oxford Dictionary of Quotations
(Oxford University Press)

The Treasury of Inspirational Anecdotes, Quotations, and Illustrations
(E. Paul Hovey)

Of course, these days, the Internet is a source of stories, illustrations, and humor; and I recommend particular websites further on in this chapter.

Other helpful resources to have on your bookshelves, and from which to draw illustrations, are compilations of short stories. I especially like the tales of Leo Tolstoy's *Walk in the Light*. Tolstoy has a great, classic style and conveys Christian values in parable form. Another volume that might be helpful in conveying spiritual truth is Edith Hamilton's *Mythology*. Ancient myths often define for us human desires and ways in which cultures have tried (and failed) to meet those needs.

My favorite source of good quotes, however, comes from books that I read by authors whom I respect and from whom I learn a great deal. As I read, I underline sentences or paragraphs that teach me or touch me. When I finish a book worth remembering, I go back and type up all the underlined passages and record the page number on which the quote is found. When I finish the several-page summary of quotes, I label it by book title and author and then file it for future reference. When the thoughts of an author have reached me, I find that those same thoughts, if expressed in exactly the same way, can reach others as well. Because I am an avid reader, these quotes become a valued resource when I want to teach others what I am learning from those who are much smarter than I am.

And, as Jo Kadlecek, master teacher and writer, says,

Read. Not just Scripture. Read the Lewises and O'Connnors, read literature, newspapers, plays, and poetry. All of these things teach about the human drama, help us to understand human beings, and help us to realize the amazing piece of literature that the Bible is. God could have just written a message in the sky, but he gave us a book containing every genre possible. We will approach the Bible differently based on our own capital—our own resources which we develop. Every teacher who is effective will be so because he has exercised his brain. Reading helps us make sense of things, helps us to appreciate language, truth.

Filing with a System

Now, what happens when you find a great story, a perfect illustration, or an insightful quotation? You might scribble it on a piece of paper and promptly lose it or put it somewhere where you will never find it again. The real key to being able to use the research and the constant scouting that you do is to make it accessible when you need it.

There may be more sophisticated ways of doing this electronically, but, for me, a simple filing system works beautifully. There are several sections to my files, as follows:

- Themes. I have a series of file folders on just about every life, biblical, and or spiritual theme you can think of. Here are some examples: Bible History, Business Management, Christmas, God as Father, Guilt, Homosexuality, Joy, Justice, Life, Meditation, Parenting, Perfectionism, Prayer, Prophecy, Redemption, Self-Esteem, Suffering, Time Management, War, Wisdom, and so on. You get the idea. If there is a topic of interest in our culture, I want to be gathering information on it. If there is a scriptural topic on which I might teach someday, I want to have a ready file of material to back up the concepts presented in Scripture. When I find a story, quote, or illustration that fits one of these themes, I print it, clip it, or copy it and drop it into the appropriate file. It is accessible quickly and easily when the subject is ripe for teaching.

- Bible. I also have sixty-six file folders in the front section of my file drawer, one for every book of the Bible. That way, when I find a good devotional insight on a passage of Scripture, I can file it either by topic or by biblical reference. I never listen to a sermon without taking notes. When I come home, I review my notes then drop them either into a Bible book file or in one of the topical files. Often, I find myself teaching through a book of the Bible. When I prepared to teach recently on Hebrews, I simply pulled my Hebrews file and culled from it material, notes, and concepts I could use in my teaching.

- Past Lessons/Messages. It is very rare that I can go back and re-use old lessons, but I keep thinking that the day will come. I enjoy learning so much and the Holy Spirit keeps giving me enough fresh material that, so far, I haven't repeated an entire lesson series. But it seems the better part of wisdom to keep them anyway. So I have drawers full (and computer disks full) of lesson series I have taught. I file them alphabetically by series title. At times, I have found myself using them for resource material for new lessons, and they offer a record of what I have researched thoroughly enough to teach. If I ever do repeat a lesson series (and I *may*, because I have some students who are asking for some refresher courses on previous series), I will probably begin with the old outlines and old assignments and, then refresh and renew the teaching until it resonates with my spirit as it is today.

- General. No filing system would be complete without some general business files. This is where I keep track of honoraria I receive, expenses I can claim against my income taxes, contracts for my writing, correspondence, thank you notes from students, new ideas for message outlines, magazine articles I am writing or have submitted, and so on (unfortunately, even rejection letters!). Your general files will be as specific to you as mine is to me, but it is a section you will need to plan for and develop.

Although you already know this, I must say one more thing in this section: Feel free to borrow freely from other authors, teachers, pastors, and even radio speakers, but always, always, *always* give credit. The way to do this best is to make careful notation of every quote, illustration,

> *Feel free to borrow freely from other authors, teachers, pastors, and even radio speakers, but always, always, **always** give credit.*

sermon outline, or devotional thought that you file. That way, you can openly use it to benefit your listeners, but at the same time attribute the source so that you are not inadvertently taking credit for someone else's work or thoughts. Not only is this an honest way of dealing with our "borrowing," but quoting others actually gives additional credibility to what we are teaching. It is helpful for our students to know that our thoughts are supportable by others who are considered experts.

Accessing Websites and Software

I am one of the last people to be acknowledged as an expert on websites, but there is a wealth of information available via the Internet that we need to be aware of. I will give you a few samples of where you might begin and, then you are on your own, but if you give this some on-line time, you will find valuable resources that are free and accessible. Besides that, they keep you from having to build an addition onto your home for a physical library to house all the information you want to have easily available! Be careful, though. You cannot assume that everything on the Internet is reliable. Make sure you either trust the source that you are researching or reading or that you corroborate information you find from more than one source.

- www.crosswalk.com and www.gospelcom.net are two websites that serve as gathering places for Christian organizations and resources. If you spend just a few minutes browsing these sites you will find web logs (blogs), daily devotionals, mission news, movie reviews, humor, feature articles, several different versions of the Bible, Bible study tools, e-cards, and links to other ministries. Both of these sites are amazing and have effectively drawn together hundreds of Christian ministries.

- www.freebiblesoftware.com will give you (for the cost of shipping and handling) a Bible software disk that includes four Bible translations, three commentaries, a Spanish Bible, a Greek Bible, Greek and Hebrew lexicons, some classic books on Christian living, systematic theology, and more.

- www.Bibles.com is the American Bible Society website through which you can order many Bible study resources and various versions of the Bible.

- www.cyberhymnal.org is an interesting site for those of us who occasionally like to quote from classic and contemporary hymns. On it, you can call up, free of charge, the words to just about any hymn you can remember the name of.

- www.christianbooks.com and www.amazon.com are great sites for ordering books and study materials. Both offer discounts, but the amount of the discount and the shipping costs vary from site to site, so I often check both to get the best value.

- *Logos Bible Study Software.* Over and over again, when I have spoken with master teachers, they mention the Logos series as the epitome in Bible study software. More information on this resource can be found at www.logos.com. Also at that site you will find a great help called "Ask the Bible." You type in your Bible study question, push the Search button, and wait for a few seconds—after which a list of related articles will be made available to you on the topic you have entered.

But getting back to the *Logos* software: There are several versions available from the Pastor's Library containing 300 volumes (cost is about $300) to the Scholar's Library containing more than 400 volumes (cost is about $1,000). The best features, though, are the research capabilities of the software. Instead of having to page through books and indices, *Logos* does it for you and produces the resources and articles that are most directly related to your research. Some teachers who have been using this software for awhile recommend strongly that purchasers enroll in a Logos user seminar (scheduled offerings are shown on their website) in order to take fullest advantage of the numerous features this comprehensive package offers.

Studying the Bible at Home

In this age of distance education, there are sources available for quality Bible study courses that we, as students, can study at home via taped lectures or via Internet delivery. This method falls short of formal seminary education but can greatly enhance the depth of our understanding of Scripture. I am familiar with two highly respected educational institutions that offer a broad array of such courses. I am sure there are others, but for purposes of sharing with you what I have personally experienced, I include these two.

* Moody Bible Institute. This well respected college in Chicago provides, in addition to its campus courses, an extensive offering of courses related to the Bible, theology, ministry, Bible study methods, and general education. The courses can be taken for undergraduate credit or can be taken for personal study only. Many are offered on-line and provide an opportunity to interact with other students as desired and with Moody professors as needed. More information can be obtained from www.moody.edu by following the icons to the independent studies site.

* Institute of Theological Studies. Located in Grand Rapids, Michigan, this organization was founded thirty years ago to provide seminary level distance education for those seeking higher level theological training. The courses, accredited by more than one hundred seminaries in the United States, are offered on CD and MP3 primarily and include a broad range of topics, such as Bible survey courses, leadership training, theology, Greek, and so on. Again, if you register through a seminary, you can get credit for these courses. But I have taken several of them on a simple audit basis which means I listen to the lectures, take notes, complete all the study questions, and read the assignments in the textbook(s). I do not submit

papers or take tests, so there's no pressure! But when I have finished a course, I have lectures I can go back to at any time for review, I have extensive notes, and I have study questions which have helped me process the material. I have found these courses to be very helpful to prepare me to teach on many biblical subjects. More information can be obtained through the ITS website at www.ITScourses.org.

Rounding Up Reference Books

If you do a lot of teaching, even if you have sophisticated computer software, there is nothing more convenient than being able to pull from the shelf a book that will immediately give you the background and understanding you need to support your presentation. There are a few that I think every teacher's library should have.

- Commentaries. Commentaries usually provide a phrase-by-phrase interpretation of the Bible from the perspective of one or more Bible scholars. Because I am not trained in original biblical languages, I rely heavily on trusted commentators to help me understand the original intention of the writers of Scripture. Two of my favorite shorter commentaries are *The Wycliffe Bible Commentary* published by Moody Press and *The Bible Knowledge Commentary* published by Victor Books. Other, more detailed commentaries can be purchased on a one-book-at-a-time basis until you have built an entire collection. One of the most accessible in terms of understanding and relevance is the "Be" series (e.g. *Be Mature, Be Comforted, Be Patient*) by Dr. Warren Wiersbe. These books cover every book in the Bible. The entire series, along with Wiersbe's expository outlines of the Old and New Testaments, are available inexpensively in CD format.

- Concordance. A concordance helps us find verses in the Bible that relate to a particular subject. A study Bible will have a concordance at the end in which we can find many subjects and many reference verses. A really valuable tool, though, is the *Strong's Exhaustive Concordance of the Bible* which lists every word used in the Bible and all the verses that use that word in the same way. This concordance also helps us locate the original Greek or Hebrew term from which the word is translated. This book is a great resource for topical teaching.

- Bible Surveys. Sometimes it is helpful to have summary versions of the books of the Bible or the themes carried throughout the Bible. There are many books that do this, but I have two favorites. The first is *Explore the Book* by J. Sidlow Baxter. Baxter has an absolute gift for seeing patterns throughout Scripture and for breaking books into outlines so that the message intended can be easily followed. The second is entitled *What the Bible is All About* and is written by Henrietta C. Mears. Mears first gives an overview of the entire Bible, then a book-by-book summary.

- Bible Encyclopedia. This resource is an alphabetical listing of terms, names, places, and so on that are found in or related to the Bible. There are many Bible encyclopedias to choose from, but my favorite is a four-volume set entitled *The International Standard Bible Encyclopedia*. There is enough detail in this publication to give sufficient background on the subject chosen, but not so much as to bog us down as we do our research. This is a very user-friendly and helpful set, published by William B. Eerdmans.

- Topical Bible. From my early beginning in Bible study, a favorite tool has been *Nave's Topical Bible* (Moody Press). This resource is used like a concordance to look up the name or word that you are researching. But, instead of finding references, Nave's actually prints out the verses in which the word appears. So we do not find ourselves flitting through the Bible to find out if the reference is apropos to the teaching we are doing. Instead, the verses are printed in paragraph form and ready for us to peruse. This is a real time saver.

Please note that many of these volumes have editions that relate to various versions of the Bible. When you are ready to purchase any of them, double check to see if you need the one that is suited to the New International Version, New King James Version and so on, depending on the one that you most frequently use for your study.

Sprucing Up Your Speaking Skills

When I am teaching my intimate classes on Saturday mornings or weekday evenings, I do not have a confidence crisis in the public-speaking category. My students are enthusiastic, patient, and supportive, so I just go at it and they accept me just as I am. When I am asked to speak to a larger group, though, mainly of people I do not know well, then I brush up on my public-speaking skills and secretly wish that I had the public presentation charisma of Oprah Winfrey. In reality, the best way to learn to speak is by speaking, but in order to make sure that we are not just practicing (and getting good at) really bad speaking habits, it is wise to submit ourselves to some more formal speech training. There are several good resources for this.

- Speak UP With Confidence. This is a helpful Christian-speaking seminar that I have taken and profited from. The basic seminar covers a Thursday evening, Friday evening, and full day Saturday and provides speech instruction and then opportunity to give prepared speeches in a small group setting. Feedback is provided after each speech is given, so the participants learn not only from their own presentations but also from the feedback given to others on their speeches. A more advanced seminar covers a similar time frame, uses more in-depth materials, and includes a preaching/professional speaking track option. The course is taught by Carol Kent, a well known author and speaker at Christian women's conferences, and others.

- Toastmasters Club. There are more than 10,000 Toastmasters Clubs in ninety countries around the world. These clubs usually consist of fifteen to thirty members who meet once a week to practice public-speaking skills. Impromptu speeches are given each week on an assigned topic and prepared speeches are given as well. The group provides to each individual helpful feedback and encouragement. Many have indicated this group to be a good confidence booster. Fees are very low, attendance at every meeting is not mandatory, and pressure is minimal. For more information, try www.toastmasters.org.

- Dale Carnegie Courses. This course is much more intense than either Speak UP or Toastmasters, but the results have been highly acclaimed for years. I have not taken the Dale Carnegie Courses, but I have friends and business associates who have and applaud the results. The basic Carnegie course meets for one night a week (three-and-a-half-hour sessions) for twelve weeks. There are textbooks to read and speeches to prepare. The sessions include the presentations of speeches, group activities, and teaching by trained Carnegie instructors. Emphasis is on building relationship and presentation skills. You can learn more at www.dalecarnegie.com. If you are employed full-time, you might even check to see if your employer would reimburse the tuition cost if you successfully complete the course. Many businesses encourage their employees to expand their confidence and presentation abilities by taking one or more of these courses.

- Books. It's hard to believe we can learn to speak by reading a book, but I do think the written text can be of help. Of course, that may be because I am a certified bibliophile, but you probably have already figured that out by now. Two speech books that have been helpful to me include *How to Say It with Your Voice* by Fortune 500 speech coach Jeffrey Jacobi. As the title implies, this book actually gives voice exercises as well as pronunciation and enunciation tips in order to help speakers express themselves clearly, effectively, and confidently. The second is entitled *The Lost Art of the Great Speech* and is written by award-winning speechwriter Richard Dowis. This book is more about the preparation and organization of the speech and includes presentation advice, as well. There are, in fact, many books on this subject. It is fun sometimes just to browse the shelves at Barnes & Noble or Borders and pick one to encourage or refresh our speechmaking abilities.

We live in an information age, so resources abound. My advice is to do some research, choose a few that work for you and your teaching style, and get to know them well. Then, expand beyond those few as time allows and as your need for growth calls for broader study. I trust, though, that the information provided in this chapter will give you a start in sorting through the myriad sources available today.

Then remember that we can have all the information in the world available to us and still miss the target if we are not sensitive to the needs of our students and not submissive to the leadership of the Holy Spirit in our teaching. The Bible is still our best and primary resource. The rest are just points of light to help us understand it better.

 Let's Review and Evaluate

So, how does our library grow?

Do we make space in our homes for books that are specifically related to teaching the Bible? Are we systematically building that library so that resources will be at our fingertips?

Are we stretching ourselves to become Internet savvy and make effective use of the many resources available through the worldwide web?

Are we seeking stories, illustrations, and quotes in our day-to-day lives and then filing them in a way that is retrievable when we need them?

Are we continuing to expand our minds and our abilities to think and to communicate by reading on a broad range of subjects?

Are we polishing our public-speaking and presentation skills so that, when the Holy Spirit speaks through us, our students don't have difficulty hearing him?

TEN

TIPS FROM
MASTER TEACHERS

What makes authentic disciples is not visions, ecstasies, biblical mastery of
chapter and verse, or spectacular success in the ministry,
but a capacity for faithfulness.

—Brennan Manning in *The Ragamuffin Gospel*

Master Bible teachers give advice in the next few pages on some of these
topics:

- Building a vital relationship with God.
- Enjoying and fostering lifelong learning.
- Preparing and presenting life-changing lessons.
- Interacting authentically with students.
- Finding opportunities to get hands-on teaching experience.

Jesus himself set up a discipleship/teaching model when he lived
with and taught those closest to him. If we follow the sequence
in the Gospels, we find that he spent considerable amount of time
and effort in directly teaching them what they needed to know. The
Sermon on the Mount takes up three full chapters in Matthew's account,
and that is only one of the formal instruction sessions. We know there
were many other teaching moments between Jesus and his disciples as
they walked along the road, sat around the campfire at night, or shared
meals. As we have already seen, John devotes three chapters in his book

to the specific teaching Jesus gave at the last supper he had with his disciples before he was arrested and killed. In addition to the formal and informal teaching, he modeled for them the lessons he taught. He was kind, compassionate, powerful, wise, and discerning; and they saw all this as they watched him interact with those he encountered day by day.

At one point, we find that Jesus is ready to send his twelve disciples out for a trial run to see if they can put into practice what he was teaching them. First, he gave them authority to drive out evil spirits and to heal sickness. Then he gave them explicit instructions about going from town to town, how they were to prepare (really *not* to prepare), what they were to do when they got to each new venue (preach, heal, drive out demons), and how they were to find places to stay and food to eat. He gave them some warnings and some reassurances and then sent them on their way.

Luke reports that they returned from their travels and reported to Jesus what they had done. We are not given details on this meeting, but I can just imagine their telling Jesus about their successes and failures and Jesus responding with encouragement, advice, and further instruction. That is what a teacher does. He teaches, he allows the student a trial run, and then he re-teaches to make sure the lesson is learned and that the student can continue to grow in his learning and in putting that learning into practice.

Later, we find that Jesus expands his teaching influence by sending out seventy-two (for those of you who are sticklers for detail, some versions say seventy) disciples to be frontrunners for him in the towns that he himself was going to visit. Again, he gave specific instructions and empowered them to have victory over evil spirits and diseases. And, as in the sending out of the twelve, we find the seventy-two returning to Jesus and reporting to him on the journey they had taken and the ministry they had undertaken.

By the time Jesus left this earth to return to heaven, he knew that numerous followers were trained and at least somewhat experienced in sharing the message of the Gospel. Additionally, he knew that the coming Holy Spirit would complete the teaching he had begun and would supernaturally empower his emissaries to take the Gospel message around the world.

We find the leaders of the early church following closely in this teaching pattern that Jesus had established. Paul traveled to new areas, taught the truths that Jesus had taught, and established fledgling congregations of new believers. He left them with Old Testament Scriptures and the insights he had given. But he didn't leave them forever. He kept teaching them, correcting their errors, and keeping them growing in their faith and understanding. He accomplished this ongoing training by return visits, by sending other church leaders to meet with them, and by writing letters. He taught, he gave some time for the teaching to work in their lives, and then he followed up.

All Bible teachers, at times, are like Jesus, or Paul, or the early church leaders in that we teach, we shepherd those who are still learning, and we follow up to ensure that our students are applying correctly what we have taught. There are other times when we are the learners and we can put ourselves in the position of gleaning knowledge and insights from those who have gone before us, who have more practical experience than we have, and who are willing to share from their storehouse of wisdom.

The purpose of this chapter is to present some such gleanings from master teachers who have been kind enough to share their wisdom with us. I have reviewed the interviews conducted, have sorted the advice or tips given by the master teachers, and have grouped the tips into categories in order to provide ten key guides to enable us to become better and better in our ability to communicate God's Word and his message to the students who learn from us.

Here, then, is a summary of the top ten teaching tips that master teachers have provided:

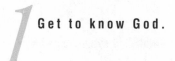

1 Get to know God.

Some pundit once said that a good lawyer knows the law but a really great lawyer knows the judge. I know that the statement is facetious, but I think there is something we can learn from it. We can know the Bible inside out and backwards, but if we don't know God, we are teaching facts and stories and our teaching is not going to change lives. None of us wants to be merely a noisemaker. We want to be effective change agents in the lives of those who look to us for leadership and for understanding.

The key to power in our teaching is being connected to the Giver of that power. Paul, one of the master teachers of all times, put it this way, "I consider everything a loss compared to the surpassing greatness of knowing Christ Jesus my Lord, for whose sake I have lost all things …" (Philippians 3:8a). These words came after he pronounced a litany of all he had learned academically and the strict teachings he had followed as a young boy growing up in a well educated, conservative, observing Jewish home. He knew more than most about the written Scriptures, his Jewish heritage, and the demands of the synagogue upon his life. He followed those requirements to the letter. Yet, when he met Jesus, his life was turned upside down and everything that he had learned and practiced without knowing the Messiah he discarded. Now the only thing that mattered was knowing and following Jesus.

We are teaching God's Word and presenting God's message. How foolish we would be to think that we could present the facts without knowing personally the one who wrote the book from which we teach. When it comes to teaching spiritual truths, knowing God is more important than anything else.

Here is what some of the master teachers say:

Obedience is the organ of spiritual knowledge. God teaches those who are submitted to him and ready to obey. To teach what we aren't living ourselves is hypocrisy. Also, we must depend on the Spirit for guidance. To be "teacher-taught" is one thing; to be "Spirit-taught" is quite something else.

—Dr. Warren Wiersbe

Obviously, the givens are keeping your own walk with God dynamic, personal, and intimate.

—Rev. William Dondit

Spiritually I prepare with a daily devotional life and I offer each presentation to God before it is delivered to the people. Prayer and reflection are key.

—Dr. Ravi Zacharias

I ask him to show me things, as I study, that I would miss without his enlightenment. When I have opportunity to teach, I try to slow down to ask, "Is this what you want me to teach, Lord, now?"

—Kathleen O. Sindorf

It is my goal to develop a real and growing relationship with the Lord. I do this through a Bible reading plan and a memorization plan. By following these, I get into the Word in a way that is separate from studying for preaching or teaching. I want the Word of God to come to my heart before I preach it.

—Dr. Don Denyes

I believe that prayer is primarily connecting with God, it is drawing near to God for fellowship and yieldedness. It is making the most of his presence as we learn to enjoy him and rest in his goodness.

—Dr. Erwin Lutzer

2 Never stop learning.

Teachers are natural students. One of the reasons we like to teach is that we like to learn, and teaching provides us an outlet of all the good things we take in. But, many of the master teachers caution against becoming so absorbed in teaching our curriculum or our Bible lesson that we become oblivious to the culture around us or to great works of art and literature that provide insight into the human condition. These experienced teachers encourage us to read widely, to foster a healthy curiosity about the created world, and continually to be aware of problems that people face day by day. Newspapers are one source of current information. In years past, I would occasionally indulge in the purchase of the *New York Times*, just to get a viewpoint different from that in my hometown paper. My husband reads the *Wall Street Journal* faithfully and passes on to me an occasional article or op ed piece that he thinks would be of interest to me or of help in my teaching.

Learning can come through reading, as we have said. But, we should not just read the Bible or Christian authors. We should challenge and sharpen our thinking by reading some authors with whom we disagree. Even television can offer such a mental challenge if we look for it. Book TV (C-Span) or PBS offer interviews with authors or documentaries on philosophies and worldviews that broaden our understanding of how the unbelieving populace understands the world we inhabit together. We can seek out and attend public lectures in our community, visit art museums, and engage in conversations with people at work or in our social circles in order to better understand their perspectives. In listening with open mind and heart to their views, we earn the right to express our own, and the conversation may become an opportunity to share the truth of God's Word with relevance and sensitivity.

Here's what some of the master teachers say:

The context of one's preaching must deal with felt issues.

—Dr. Ravi Zacharias

I spend time studying culture through media, magazines, and interacting with key leaders through their writing. At the same time, I study Scripture. My job as a minister is to bridge the two by bringing in appropriate application of scriptural concepts in my teaching.

—Dr. Don Denyes

I read a wide variety of Christian books and secular books as spiritual and intellectual preparation. I try to be a student of people and a student of culture.

—Dr. Bill Rudd

One of the key ways to make the truth of the Gospel relevant is to know the culture. We don't have to be afraid of it or retreat from it. Instead we can actually engage it. If God is who he says he is, we don't have to be reticent about that. First we need to understand culture, then just be ourselves. We engage it with our lives. We have a rich heritage—J. R. R. Tolkein, C. S. Lewis, Flannery O'Connor—really smart people who believed this, articulated it, and then had an impact on culture. We have to continue the hard work of thinking things through.

—Jo Kadlecek

I find that if I am at a period in my life when I cannot read a lot, it affects my vocabulary and ability to deliver in the classroom. Reading shapes my mind, ideas flow when I read a lot and on a wide variety of subjects.

—Dr. Rex Rogers

3 Love people.

Those of us who love to learn need also to learn to love. We need to sometimes get out of our quiet studies and away from our computer research into the real world. We need to understand what people are watching on television, what they are talking about at neighborhood parties, what they read in newspapers, and what they are worried about. The Great Commandment is given in two parts: Love God and love your neighbor. In reality, it is simply the command to love. If we love God, we *will* love our neighbors. As teachers, we need to let that love grow and let it show to those around us. Then our teaching will grow out of a true understanding of and caring for those who come to listen and learn.

> Those of us who love to learn need also to learn to love.

As one master teacher stated, "Love your students; everything else will fall into place." For those of us who are used to studying, preparing, analyzing, and presenting, that advice may sound too simple. Yet, without a sincere love for those we teach, we will accomplish nothing of value in their lives. As Paul said, "If I speak with human eloquence and angelic ecstasy but don't love, I'm nothing but the creaking of a rusty gate. If I speak God's Word with power, revealing all his mysteries and making everything plain as day … but I don't have love, I'm nothing" (I Corinthians 13:1–2 *The Message*).

The bottom line, though, is that the kind of love we are talking about here is God-given. It is being able to love those who are not always lovable, those who are not like us, those who are most in need of God's transforming touch. For that kind of love, we go to the Lover of our own souls. God himself will fill us with *agape* as we invite him to do so, as we sense the great love he has for us, and as we allow him to use us as conduits of his love to others. Loving that deeply and that unselfishly will put us at risk of being hurt, of showing compassion we didn't know we had, and of costing us a great deal in terms of time and material possessions. But **great teachers are great lovers**. We dare not be less.

Here's what some of the master teachers say:

I have seen students' lives change because I loved them. I don't change them, love does.

—Dr. Tamara Rosier

Many love teaching, they love the Word, they love parsing verbs, they love being before a crowd, they love being innovative, but fail to love people. These are the kind who crawl out from under a rock (their study) once a week, deliver their message, and then crawl back under their rock with a "just don't bother me" attitude. My tip: You must LOVE people. I see the absence of that on a large scale.

—Rev. Bill Dondit

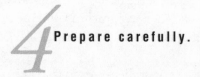

4 Prepare carefully.

It takes a lot of time, thought, and prayer to put together a lesson or a message that will impact the lives of the students we teach. But the master teachers I talked to say that preparation must always be done with the listeners in mind. What do we want them most to remember? How do we illustrate that most important point so that it will be memorable to them? How do we engage their minds so that they respond with a logical, progressing thought process? How do we make sure that they have opportunity to mentally process the information they are taking in?

All of this takes careful planning *and* a great deal of discarding. That is one of the most difficult jobs to me as I prepare to teach: throwing out the extras, the peripheral, and the side roads. It is important to stick to the main points and to lead our students along the path of thought so that we and they all end up at the same place. It is too easy to interrupt the flow of their thinking by overloading them with detail or impressing them with all we know.

Lack of preparation and over preparation can both be serious teaching errors. I know teachers who claim reliance on the Holy Spirit and go into a classroom ready to "wing it." This approach is not actually teaching. It is really just spending an hour or so with a class. Just being together for discussion will result in some good, but, as teachers, we are responsible for much more than that. We must be prepared both in our understanding of the subject and in our planned presentation to a specific audience. As we prepare our lessons, we need to be thinking of the listeners at every step of the way, at every point of the outline. If we love them, we will meet them where they are and lead them further along the road to spiritual growth and health.

Here's what some of the master teachers say:

Do not ramble along, changing topics as you meander through the text. You need to have coherence—unity, order, and progress are essential to the teaching process.

—Dr. Erwin Lutzer

I came at teaching like an academic study—with twelve pages of notes. I overwhelmed my audiences with information. I have found that I need to spend enough time figuring out how to illustrate main points as I do in the study/research phase. I have to help my students connect the dots. It's more than learning information.

—Dr. Rex Rogers

Don't over prepare because, if you do, you will over teach. You will be thinking you have to get through all the material. But your role is really that of facilitator. In order to facilitate effectively, you have to leave time for processing before you teach, during the teaching, and after the lesson.

—Dr. Tamara Rosier

Be careful to teach what it is saying in the text and context and not ride hobbyhorses to drive home your own agenda. My professor of Old Testament at Trinity used to say two things. "Keep your finger on the text," and of a sermon that didn't do that he would say, "Great sermon, poor text," meaning thereby, "Some fine thoughts here, but that's not what the text is intending or stating."

–Dr. Ravi Zacharias

5 Present your lesson with enthusiasm and conviction.

Because I teach and speak, I make it a practice to listen to other speakers as often as possible. Some are on tape or CD and others are in classes I take or lectures I attend. If they are good communicators, I often evaluate afterwards what it was that they did so well. Without exception, the greatest speakers are those who convey their message as if they really believe it and convince me of the importance of their message by their energy and enthusiasm. Style isn't everything, but it is important. We have the greatest news in the world and our delivery should reflect our enthusiasm for that message. Master teachers encourage us to be animated, energetic, and upbeat. Our students should sense that we are excited about what we have learned and about what we want to share with them. It is as if we have an awesome secret and we are letting them in on it. Gestures help as do stories, facial expressions, and voice variations.

The only way to be that genuinely enthusiastic is to truly believe in the importance of what we have to say. Most of the master teachers I spoke to commented on the need to craft a message with the transformation of the student in mind. Once we know why our teaching matters, the desire to pass the message along to those who need it most will drive the energy of our presentation.

Here is what some of the master teachers say:

I always ask myself, "Why should anyone be changed because of what I teach or preach?" I tell young preachers that every sermon should answer these questions: "What burning issues are you answering that people should be asking?" and "After you are finished, would people feel free to come and discuss the topic with you?" and "Why should anyone's life be changed forever because of this message or your teaching?"

—Dr. Erwin Lutzer

One of my favorite expressions is, "I want my students to 'own' the material." I am most concerned that those I am teaching, regardless of what they have brought to the classroom by way of experience, maturity, prior knowledge, et cetera, will leave the classroom (or at least by the end of the semester) changed persons—that the material of the course will have somehow been wedded to their own intellectual DNA, and that they not simply leave more knowledgeable about an idea, a topic, a biblical principle, … but that this has had some impact or effect on how they both think and how they intend to live.

—Dr. Ron Mahurin

Saturate yourself in the text you are going to teach. Read it multiple times. G. Campbell Morgan would read a text fifty times before he preached it. It is important that you are familiar enough with the passage that it becomes a part of you. Then you will teach with passion, you will teach from your heart, not your head. Truth and insight passionately delivered are the real burden of teaching.

—Dr. Don Denyes

In each class it is my goal to teach the lesson (the "what?"), help them to see the significance (the "so what?") and encourage them to make application of the lesson to their lives (the "now what?").

—Dr. Tamara Rosier

We must relate our material to what our audience is thinking about or living. We need to help people do moral reasoning on issues. We get Christian kids from Christian homes who can quote Bible verses but cannot tell the relevance of a Bible story to today. Christ taught so people could "get it."

—Dr. Rex Rogers

6 Interact authentically with your students.

A generation ago teaching was lecturing. The teacher talked, the students listened and took notes. Then, at some point after the lecture, the students were asked, via a test or discussion, to recite back to the teacher what they had been taught. It doesn't work that way anymore. Master teachers are strong in their observation that real teaching today involves interaction between student and teacher. The best teachers see themselves as facilitators, those who present ideas for intellectual and spiritual processing by the students. Master teachers assume their students have good thinking power and are able, with some guidance, to assimilate information, process its significance, and apply it appropriately to their lives.

Another common thread I picked up from master teacher comments was that, when interaction is encouraged in the classroom, students become teachers. Because of the enlightenment given by the Holy Spirit and because of the individual life experiences that each participant in a discussion brings to the table, we learn from one another. The presenter has a responsibility to bring in thoughts, ideas, data, application, and biblical teaching, but the real learning (sometimes for both teacher and student) comes in when there is an opportunity to process those concepts through verbalization, feedback, and interaction.

A third concept that master teachers commented on regarding interaction was the teacher's authenticity. Students want to relate to a real person, someone who faces the same difficulties they do, but maybe is just further along the road in understanding how to deal with those difficulties. We must be willing to be vulnerable, to share stories from our own lives, and to admit weaknesses and failures. I did this in class just last week and received a follow-up note from one of my students which said, in part, "Thanks for sharing from your heart and personal experience. It reminds us that you are real. You have struggles and trials of your own. We tend to be misled and think that if we 'get it right' like you, life will be easier. The saints in the Bible are always great to learn from, but we also need saints of the here and now that we can see and touch."

Here's what some of the master teachers say about interaction and authenticity:

When I teach, I absolutely need interaction. I believe that all teachers and preachers have to have what I call 'connectedness'; that is, they need to connect with people if they want to communicate. It is not enough to give out content, there must be transformation, and you can only do that when you win the person over to yourself. If they like you, they will learn. If they don't, it doesn't matter much how great your lectures are.

—Dr. Erwin Lutzer

The true teacher must be himself/herself and not imitate somebody else. Teach the message God gives you and do it your way. The listener who doesn't like my approach may respond enthusiastically to your approach.

—Dr. Warren Wiersbe

I like to pose questions and get people thinking. I search for issues and lead discussions with my students, encouraging them to discover truths for themselves … I challenge them to think and then to discuss how to apply the learning with what they are going through. God speaks through His Word and through other people, too. We enlighten one another.

—Kathleen O. Sindorf

If we are acting on God's behalf, we need to be need-meeters for our students. Teaching begins with an authentic relationship. We need to let them know we're human. Sharing personal stories is one way to do that. The brain works to learn when it is feeling safe.

—Dr. Tamara Rosier

The best qualification for teachers of the Word is their ability to use story to help communicate things. Along with that is their willingness to be honest, real, and personal about their communication. If our own story is not integrated into the story of Scripture, we will not be as effective as teachers.

—Jo Kadlecek

It really is a combination of argument and story that bridges the head to the heart, appealing then to the will.

—Dr. Ravi Zacharias

Know your audience.

The best way to get to love our students and to interact authentically with them is to get to know them. Many master teachers mentioned the importance of spending time with them inside and outside the classroom. A lunch meeting, a social time, a little gift, a cup of coffee, a shared book, a listening ear, a sympathetic pat on the shoulder—all these are ways to reach into our students' lives, and that kind of reaching out will encourage relationship that will grow into love. Jesus looked at people and loved them. We usually have to get to know people to love them, so, as master teachers, we are wise to invest the time and effort into knowing and loving our students.

That kind of knowledge will guide our teaching. We will choose our topics with our students' needs in mind, we will pray over them as we open God's Word to teach them, we will be able to put lessons together in a way that will be relevant to their lives, and, most importantly of all, the love will show in our voices, our faces, and our words as we unfold God's truths to them day after day.

Here's what some of the master teachers say:

At church and in other settings, the topics are often shaped by conversations with those who are in leadership, trying to assess the particular needs of a congregation, campus, or other group, and tailoring what I can bring to the particular needs of the community.

—Dr. Ron Mahurin

Know your audience as well as you possibly can before you plan your lesson. Do they like humor or think it silly and a waste of time? Do they need an example to make points clear? Do they like to interact with you or just listen?

— Phyllis Nye

8 Direct your focus.

It is very hard to stand up in front of a group of people and not be concerned about what they think of us. How do we look? Will they like us? Will they want to come back to hear more? But, the more we focus on ourselves and the image we are projecting, the more anxious we will become and the less effective our teaching will be.

Master teachers have learned to focus on two things: their students and their message. Our minds can hold only so many thoughts at one time. If they are filled with thoughts about our audience and our lesson, there will be no room for anxious thoughts that will detract both us and our students from what we have to say.

I find that if I really believe that my audience needs to hear the message I am about to give and if I have interacted with my text long enough and deeply enough that it begins to affect my own life, then I am less likely to be worried about my outward appearance or the students' acceptance of me. When I am preparing, I try to keep up my research and study until I find something in the lesson that excites me, that challenges me, and that changes me. When that happens, I am ready to teach it to someone else.

Here's what some of the master teachers say:

I don't want my presentation to be an academic experience. It needs to be kneaded into me so it becomes part of my experience. If it's not real to me, no one will care what I have to say.

—Jo Kadlecek

In teaching God's Word, I want to draw the listeners into that space and place where they must wrestle with the realities of the brokenness of our world, and at the same time, the loving grace that God extends to us in Christ. And I desire that they seek to go out into a culture that desperately needs that message of love and grace—and are able to present that message in winsome ways that will invite others to want to know more about who Jesus is, and why his claims on our lives are so revolutionary.

—Dr. Ron Mahurin

Let the truth change you and then pray that it will change others.

—Dr. Erwin Lutzer

The conviction can only come from the Holy Spirit. I jokingly say that I am not skilled in Power Point. I lean on him for the power as I try to make the point.

—Dr. Ravi Zacharias

Most anxiety comes from worrying about what other people will think of us. If we force our minds to think about the audience and their needs and to think about the message that we are giving, then we will not have room in our minds to think about what they are thinking of us.

—Kathleen O. Sindorf

9 Get experience.

Teaching is a developed gift. It is a rare teacher who is a smashing success the first time he or she teaches. For most of us, it is a learning process that requires many months and years of practice. I think back on my first year of teaching high school literature. I tried hard, and I connected with a few students, but my teaching was marginal, at best. My second year was better than my first, though, and by the third year, things were going pretty well. Still, I would teach poetry a lot differently today from how I did then!

If you have taught for any length of time, I am sure you have had a similar experience. And I assume you are reading this book because you want to get better at what you do. Many of the master teachers told stories of teaching neighborhood kids in the backyard in their pre-adolescent years. Others told of grabbing every opportunity to teach younger children in Sunday School classes or to preach in country churches or at rescue missions. I taught high school completion English classes in nursing homes for a few years when my children were young and I wanted only part-time work. Great memories and great learning moments grew out of that unique experience.

Every teaching opportunity is a learning opportunity for us. It is important that we look for venues in which to grow our teaching skills by being willing to teach in some less-than-glamorous situations. Sometimes those are the places where we are needed most!

Here's what some of the master teachers say:

I learned that it is fun to teach someone else and fun to work together in the learning process … Through the years, the Lord began to open up opportunities for me to teach.

—Kathleen O. Sindorf

Be willing to recognize small beginnings and humbling settings.

—Dr. Ravi Zacharias

I took every opportunity I had to speak and to teach.

—Dr. Don Denyes

During my sophomore year in college, I talked to my dad (who was a dentist) about the possibility of changing my major so I could go into medicine. He agreed to support me whatever I decided to do, but he said, "Don't forget that God has given you a gift." I prayed about my decision. Then I knew that if I couldn't preach, I didn't want to live. By the time I graduated from college, I had as much preaching and teaching experience as some who had been serving as pastors for five years.

—Dr. Bill Rudd

I see teaching as a responsibility, not a right. I am a servant in that classroom. That means that I want to do a good job. I pray, asking for God's blessing over each student. I pray that solid relationships will be built as I meet with my class to prepare them to teach. This is a holy time for them. I know the course content, but the spiritual preparation is essential. At the end of each semester, I feel blessed to have been able to teach. I am not in teaching for the power; instead, teaching is my offering.

—Dr. Tamara Rosier

Enjoy!

My husband and I were sitting at the table one day last spring sharing our early morning cup of coffee. The birds were singing, the sun was shining, new green leaves were beginning to come out on the trees. Our cat was on the back of the couch in the next room observing the squirrels spiraling up and down the trees. As Warren looked around at the scene we were part of, he commented quietly, "It just doesn't get any better than this."

That's exactly the way I feel some God-blessed days when I stand in front of a group of people who are eager to learn, who respond well to the teaching, and who begin to show that what they are learning is affecting their lives and their relationships. "It just doesn't get any better than this!"

Teaching is hard work, but it is rewarding work. When we think of what we learn ourselves, the spiritual growth we attain because we are connected to God through the study of his Word, and the friendships we make with our fellow learners, our hearts are overwhelmed with thanksgiving and joy. God gives us the gift of teaching, he calls us to use it to further his kingdom, and he gives us joy as we do just that. The master teachers I talked to expressed that enjoyment in many different ways, but they all acknowledged that teaching is a privilege that comes with many rewards. When Jesus came, he promised abundant life to his followers. For me, for you, and for our comrades in the ministry of teaching, sharing God's truths with others provides just that. He meant for us to enjoy what we do for him.

Here's what some of the master teachers say:

Study has also been a means of developing the gift along with the sheer joy that comes from teaching, especially when you see the life-changing effect your teaching has had on someone.

—Rev. William Dondit

One of the best experiences I have had in teaching is being able to participate for the past six years as a teacher at the Fellowship of Christian Athletes women's leadership retreat in Southern California. Every year we have the same worship leader, me as a teacher, and the same people coming bringing new friends. The vision is to build community, not just to have a conference. It's all of us together. They have seen me grow as much as I have seen them grow. I have developed really close friendships because of that.

—Jo Kadlecek

I could tell by the look on a few faces when I had made a connection. They would just light up! Then I would double back and pick up the faces that were not lit until they could get it, too. It was a real joy to see them put into action something I had taught.

—Phyllis Nye

Teaching is a form of spiritual discipline because it is a sacred trust. Having to teach forces you into Scripture. You always learn more than the recipients of your teaching.

—Dr. Rex Rogers

If we are called to teach God's Word, then we must teach. We will not be content to do anything less. But, we will never be experts at anything as Spirit driven as teaching God's message. So we begin where we are, we work hard to learn, we allow the Holy Spirit to make his message real in our lives, and then we teach out of a heart of passion for God and love for our students. We begin with the opportunities in front of us and we allow God to grow us, to guide us, and to use us as simple instruments in his hand. We are to be faithful to God and faithful to the text that we teach. When we are, the results are up to the One who has called us——and the rewards are eternal.

Appendix I

Roadmap to Successful Teaching

The chart on the next two pages will help you visually navigate through the process of teaching, from the initial call to seeing the end results of changed lives. At each step, appropriate reference is given to the chapter in *The Bible Study Teacher's Guide* that will best help in developing the particular skill needed.

The Nudge

You have a desire to learn and then to share what you are learning. You are beginning to sense that this desire may have been planted by God and that you are, in fact, called to teach his Word to those who want to learn. More about the call to teach is given in **Chapter 1**.

The Preparation

Where do you go from here? Are you personally ready to teach? Are you spiritually ready? Do you have a message to give?

The Messenger

Most of the preparation at this point needs to be of the heart. Have you submitted to the authority of God's Word in your life? Are you living a life of purity and commitment to him? Help is given in **Chapter 2**.

The Message

You choose a topic, review materials, glean main points, seek God's guidance, formulate an outline, and prepare your lesson. Practical guidance is given in **Chapter 3**.

Resources

Information is readily available for teachers; sometimes you just need to know where to look. Resource help is provided in **Chapter 9**.

Warnings

Be aware of the points of danger for teachers: criticism, pride, hard work, stresses, temptation, accountability. If you know what to look for, you can be prepared! **Chapter 8** will help.

Tips

Many have walked this path before you and, as master teachers, are willing to share tips that will help you master your craft and avoid pitfalls along the way. See **Chapter 10**.

The Presentation

Prepare to present yourself and your message well. Practice good skills by being enthusiastic, using eye contact, carrying yourself with confidence, and sincerely engaging your audience. Lots of helps on this topic are given in **Chapter 4**.

Connecting

The goal is not just presenting good material, but seeing lives transformed by the messages we give from God's Word. We must know our students and make sure our message relates to their lives. **Chapter 5** will give you some great tips on how to do this with effectiveness.

Discussion

Interaction with students is a must, and lively discussion is the best way to draw them into the learning process. There are ways that work and ways that don't. See **Chapter 6** for some helpful guidelines.

Mentoring

Some teachers never teach in front of a large group, but are changing lives one at a time. Jesus was a great mentor, and we can follow his example. If you have an opportunity to build one-on-one into the life of another person, **Chapter 7** and **Appendix II** will be of help.

APPENDIX II

Sample Mentoring Curriculum

In the following pages, I give you some examples of the types of things Darla and I (my friend from Chapter 7) talked about as we met together. Obviously, this plan was written for a woman who is a full-time wife and mother and who has financial resources to make her life work with efficiency. While these qualities are specific to Darla's situation, my hope is that these notes might give you ideas of how you can mentor another individual, following a pattern like this one or creating one that is particularly suited for your mentee's needs.

Unit One: Home

Decorating:
Creating a warm and welcoming home environment

1. *Conduct an assessment.*
Walk through each room of the house with a notepad. Write down anything you see that could make an improvement in visual appeal. Think of things like color choices, arrangement of furniture, wall art, clutter, etc. Begin with the most used room of the house and, one at a time, make the changes that you have written on your list.

2. *Engage the services of a decorator.*
Ask him/her to assess your home and create a five-year plan for updating and improving the décor. Begin to shop for the items suggested and to make improvements over the next several years to create the atmosphere in your home that you and your family will enjoy.

Management:
Overseeing the smooth operation of your household

1. *Conduct an assessment.*
Walk through each room of the house again with a notepad. Write down anything you see that needs repair or replacement. Observe the condition of walls and woodwork as well as furnishings, light fixtures, etc. Make a master list of repair and replacement items that you need to work on.

2. *Create a master list of service providers.*
Have at your fingertips, either on the computer or on note cards, the

following service providers' names, addresses, and contact information: appliance repair, pool service, lawn service, snow plowing, handyman, insurance agent, roof/exterior services, locksmith, heating/cooling service, plumber, electrician, tree trimmer, housekeeper, and any others that you may use regularly or that may be unique to your home.

3. *Oversee repairs.*
Complete the simple repairs that you or your family members can make. Call for help on the others and oversee the repair to your satisfaction. Cultivate relationships with the key service providers by being friendly, tipping if appropriate, and paying on time. The extra effort this takes will pay big dividends in an emergency situation.

4. *Keep accurate records.*
Create a home maintenance file in which you keep warranties, service records, owner's manuals, and other operating and troubleshooting information.

Organization:
Preparing in advance to avoid unnecessary stresses

1. *Conduct an assessment.*
Look carefully at each room of your house for which you are responsible (e.g. children's rooms and husband's office may not be yours to organize!). Your bedroom, the bathrooms, the mudroom/laundry room, the office, and the kitchen are probably your main arenas for focus. List the most obvious problem areas of disorganization with others following in descending order.

2. *Organize one room at a time.*
Begin with a room you can get done in a couple of hours—perhaps the master bathroom. Go through every drawer, every cupboard, and discard outdated medicines and unusable products. Clean, straighten,

reshuffle storage items as needed. Make note of items that need to be restocked. As much as possible keep counter space and furniture surfaces free of items that can be stored elsewhere. These areas should be kept clear as work spaces with other items tucked away in closets, drawers, and cupboards. Once done, move on to other rooms and closets, one at a time, until your entire house is organized. Don't be afraid to throw out unusable items or to give away outgrown or unfavored clothing and outgrown games and toys. Someone else may appreciate what your family no longer needs or wants and you will not have unneeded clutter to try to organize. Streamline and simplify!

3. *Create storage space as needed.*
Sometimes organization seems impossible because we are trying to put too much stuff in one place. Have long-term storage shelves installed in the basement or the garage or find places in your home where additional shelving or closets could be created. Remember that storage organization is essential. If you have stored it, but can't find it, you haven't accomplished your goal. Label shelves and boxes. Keep a master list in your household files of items in storage and their location.

4. *Provide for desk/office space.*
You are CEO of your home and, as such, you need a place to keep records concerning finances, time-management, shopping lists, children, medical, and house. Make sure that somewhere in your household organization, you have a place for files, for bill-paying, for letter-writing, and for record keeping.

Food:
Providing appetizing, nutritional sustenance for your family

1. *Plan weekly menus.*
Know in advance what you will prepare for each evening meal and write your grocery list based on those menus. Choose recipes that at least some of your family will enjoy, alternating to ensure that most

meals will be liked by all. Focus on variety, timely preparation, and nutrition when selecting menu items. Make sure each meal has a meat (or substitute protein), starch, vegetable, and salad. Keep dessert items on hand for members of your family who like them, but there is no need to make dessert a staple for every meal. Keep lunch items on hand, as well, for your children who carry lunches to school. Make sure there is a supply of after-school snacks that are nutritious and readily available.

2. *Grocery shop weekly.*
Keep an ongoing grocery list in a visible place in the kitchen. You can add to it when you plan your menus and your family can add to it if they use the last bottle of catsup or another staple item. Keep a pantry well stocked with such things as flour, sugar, soups, cereal, and canned goods. Keep a freezer stocked with meats, vegetables, and, for occasional use, quality prepared entrees. Try to shop no more than once a week with one stop midweek for milk, bread, and produce.

3. *Use shortcuts.*
If you find yourself overwhelmed with the cooking tasks, find good alternatives for your family. There are often catering services that will prepare entrees for you and freeze them. You can pick up several at a time to store and use as needed. There are many retail establishments now which offer two-hour-long meal-making sessions. They provide the ingredients and recipes. You pay a fee and assemble a dozen meals for your family. This is not cheating! This is making a choice to use your time effectively. Also, become familiar with prepared entrees at stores such as Gordon Food Services and Sam's Club and stock up on those that your family likes.

4. *Venture into new areas.*
Sign up for a cooking class. Better yet, go with a friend and learn cooking techniques, new recipes, and the latest in kitchen equipment. Have fun and share what you learn by surprising your family with something new and interesting!

5. *Enlist help from your family.*

The kitchen is a great place to build relationships. Encourage your children to learn to bake their favorite cookies, to participate in meal planning so that they can ensure that their best-liked foods appear on the menus often, and to help with meal preparation and clean up. There is no better place to learn teamwork, to influence the end result of their efforts, and to interact with other members of the family.

Unit Two: Children

Training:
Building in the tools for a productive, meaningful life

1. *Learn what God says about raising children.*
Read through the book of Proverbs and write out in a notebook every verse that gives instruction for raising children. Think about each one and ask God to show you how to apply it in your parenting. Memorize verses that seem especially key to your situation.

2. *Become a master teacher.*
Parents are teachers whether they realize it or not. Train yourself as a teacher by reading at least one child-rearing or family relationship book every year. Attend conferences as they become available. Find teaching opportunities in every day: life skills, relationship savvy, work habits, spiritual lessons. Teach by example, by conversation, and by direct instruction. Think of creative ways to introduce your children to new topics to investigate, new skills to master, and new thoughts to discuss.

3. *Practice fair and consistent discipline.*
All children will test boundaries to see how much freedom they have. Talk to your spouse so that you can together determine clearly what the boundaries are and then establish logical consequences for stepping across those lines. These boundaries will change as children grow but need to include such areas as respect for parents, responsible use of belongings and household goods, respectful treatment of siblings, honorable work ethic (school and/or job), and honest communication. Consequences for infractions must be applied with absolute consistency, without anger, and in love.

Interaction:
Developing family relationships that endure

1. *Create an atmosphere for community living.*
There is structure required in order for people to live together successfully in community.

(a) There are basic chores to be done:
Laundry, shopping, cleaning, food preparation, pet care, errand running, etc. Divide these chores so that each family member has an opportunity to participate in the support structure of the family. This participation will allow children to learn basic life skills that will serve them well throughout their lives. As the children mature, they should take more and more responsibility for their own welfare: mending their own clothes, cleaning their own rooms, polishing their own shoes, packing their own lunches, etc.

(b) There are basic schedules to be met:
Meals, school, work, extracurricular events. Find a way to coordinate schedules so that priorities can be met, various activities can be supported, and sharing in one another's activities can logically occur.

(c) There are basic considerations to be given:
Communication, shared equipment and facilities, courtesy, and mutual support. Develop a set of "living together" rules that include such governance items as family meetings, ride sharing, mealtimes, music volumes, television and/or computer/Internet usage, schedule prioritizations, etc. In some families, it may work better to have understandings rather than written-out rules, but some agreement should be reached as to how to live together in harmony.

2. *Find ways to enjoy one another.*

Relationships are forged in all kinds of situations, but there is nothing that builds camaraderie and love for one another like doing something fun together. Plan as a group for family vacations, movie outings, shopping expeditions, shared projects, and even a few daring adventures. Some families plan a once-a-week or monthly game night complete with favorite snacks. Others give creative birthday parties or develop a family sporting interest such as cross country skiing or hiking. Be creative, have fun together, and make happy memories!

3. *Provide a network of support for each other.*

Of course, life is not made up of just fun. There are times when the family needs to provide support for a member who is struggling. Family life must have enough down time so that listening ears can be available, quiet conversations can naturally occur, and helping hands can be lovingly offered. When one family member is hurting, all the rest need to function in supporting and nurturing roles until the crisis is past. As a parent, you will provide the example for this support and then encourage that example to be replicated in your children's relationships with one another and with you. Also, encourage the support network to be extended to healthy friendships and make sure that you know your children's friends and that they are consistently welcomed into your home.

Provision:
Meeting family members' needs

1. *Physical.*

Children have the right to know that their physical needs will be met. These needs include food, clothing, shelter, safety, medical, and other basic material provisions. In addition to being provided for, children need to be taught how to take care of the bodies that God has given. This teaching may include personal security matters, safety measures for the home, driving restrictions, nutritional and dietary guidelines, emergency home evacuation plans, call-home instructions when they are with their friends, and warnings about drugs and alcohol.

2. *Financial.*

Children should be able to expect a certain amount of financial security, knowing that their parents are able to ensure a stable lifestyle including planning ahead for their future educations. Along with this security should be a planned training program teaching them how to be fiscally responsible with the money they have. Allowances should be given with instruction for percentages to be spent, saved, and given away. Later, when children begin to earn their own incomes, similar teaching should be instilled so that giving, spending, and saving habits are firmly ingrained before a child leaves home. There are numerous books and training programs available in the marketplace today to enable parents to teach their children sound Christian financial principles. One place to check for helpful resources might be www.crown.org.

3. *Mental.*

Every parent should take seriously the role of developing the young minds in their care. Homes should be full of books, quality DVDs, and intellectually stimulating games and activities. New topics for discussion should be introduced regularly and opposing viewpoints should be encouraged. As children get older, discussions should include important social issues of the day such as abortion, homosexuality, morality, etc. Library and computer research should be encouraged. The importance of school attendance and 100 percent participation should be emphasized. Careful completion of homework must be a priority for every child every school day. Think of ways to stretch your children's minds by exposing them to new and interesting activities such as opera, ballet, music lessons, creative writing, art, missionaries, travel, etc.

4. *Emotional.*

Families can be emotionally dangerous places. Parents must find ways to protect their children from emotional onslaughts from siblings, unwitting aunts, uncles, and grandparents, and sometimes from parents themselves. Thoughtless words can cause years of hurt. Parents need to educate themselves through books and/or classes about the sensitivities of children and the necessity of nurturing them emotionally. Become a nonjudgmental listener and a sincere giver of praise. Learn to show your children total acceptance even when you have to correct inappropriate behavior. Learn to recognize signs of emotional distress in your children and get professional counseling for them if the signs do not disappear in a short period of time. Practice just being in proximity to your children and strive to be emotionally available to them on a consistent basis.

5. *Spiritual.*

There is nothing we can provide for our children that will matter one iota if we do not provide what they need for eternity: a relationship with their loving heavenly Father. Develop a spiritual formation plan for each of your children, keeping in mind their ages and their individual personalities. The plan should include discussions of spiritual principles, teaching of biblical directives, family and/or one-on-one prayer times, and church involvement. For some of your children, the plan might include finding a spiritual mentor to whom they can relate or encouraging involvement in a Bible study group or a Christian youth club at their school. Christian summer camp is a great way to give a spiritual jump start to elementary and middle school children. It may be that, in addition to these things, the most powerful tool you have in teaching your children about spiritual things is the example of your own relationship with God.

Unit Three: Husband

Respecting:
Building on his best qualities

1. *Search for the respectable.*
Search Scripture and find out what characteristics God expects from spiritual leaders. Look for those characteristics in your husband and, when you find them, thank God for them and respect your husband from the depths of your soul for exhibiting those characteristics. Focus on what he does well, and reinforce what he is that is in keeping with biblical teaching. On days when you sense that your respect for him is wavering, turn your mind to these things. Keep respect for your mate alive; one of the most fundamental needs for a man is to be respected by those he values and leads. Ephesians 5:33b: ". . . the wife must respect her husband."

2. *Express your respect in words and actions.*
Once you have established characteristics for which you respect your husband, then figure out how to show it. Your mate needs to sense and experience your respect. Communicate your respect in writing: e-mails of support, thank you cards, "thinking of you" notes, thoughtful letters on special occasions. Acknowledge his triumphs, his growth, and his value to you and to others. Make sure you are reinforcing the right things—his character, not his actions. That way, if he suffers reverses in health or wealth, he knows he can count on you to continue respecting him because your devotion is due to who he is and not to what he does or provides.

Your respect will also be communicated in how you respond to him. If he asks you to do something for him, do it unless it is something extremely unreasonable. If he makes a statement, either support it or respond with your own opinion in a well expressed and respectful way. Never use negative adjectives in addressing your husband. Never allow anger to cause you to respond disrespectfully. Even in situations when you find it hard to respect your husband as a person, show respect for the position he holds as the God-ordained head of your household. When you have engaged in any words or actions that are not respectful, acknowledge to both God and your spouse what you have done, then ask for forgiveness and restoration.

3. *Be his outspoken fan in your conversations with others.*
Knowing that others respect your husband will help you respect him, too. Do all you can to let people know the reasons that you respect and value him. Look for ways to honor him in your relationships both outside and inside the home. Never put him down in the presence of your children, either verbally or through facial expression or body language. Use every possible opportunity to build him up in the eyes of your family and friends: the way you look at him, the language you use in talking about him, the means you use in working out problems with him, and the conversations you have about him. Your respect will be evident to others and lack of it will reflect poorly on both you and him. His awareness of your speaking well of him to others will encourage him to live up to the respectable image you portray of him.

Communicating:
Expressing yourself effectively

1. *Know the message you want to give.*
The effectiveness of your communication is directly dependent upon your commitment to the message you convey. Know yourself. Know your own needs and your own strengths. And know God's standards. Then you can more capably and confidently communicate your desires, your dreams, and your very self. If you have to engage in discussion of a difficult topic, think through the issues first so that you can express them clearly. If you need to communicate about something you think the two of you will disagree on, choose your battles carefully. Not every issue needs to be addressed. Address those that are important to you personally and those that you need to come to agreement on for the

benefit of your children or others.

2. *Adapt to your husband's communication style.*

If your husband is one who likes to get to the core of the issue quickly, try to make your point accordingly. Choose a time that is good for discussion. Is he more open in the morning or at the end of the day? Choose a place that is good for discussion. Do you need to get away from distractions by going out for coffee or escaping to the den or the bedroom? Remember that your body language, facial expressions, and tone of voice usually communicate more than your words. Endeavor to make all of these aspects of communication consistent with the message you want to convey and with the style in which your spouse best receives and understands your message.

3. *Listen interactively.*

Learning the art of good listening will benefit all of your relationships, but especially your marriage. Listen for the real message that the speaker is trying to communicate. Read between the lines by mentally recalling past conversations and the history of your relationship. Observe emotional tone, voice, and body language. Ask good questions. Focus on his need. Listen without interruption until the entire message is conveyed. Respond in love and understanding. Repeat back to him in your own words what you thought he was saying to you. Allow him to correct any misunderstanding you may have. If you do not agree with a conclusion he has reached or cannot meet a request he is making, counter graciously and rationally. Good listening requires patience, alertness, and sensitivity.

4. *Build communication into your schedule.*

There is nothing as important to a strong relationship as communication. So, make time for it consistently. Find ten or fifteen minutes daily to sit together, maybe over coffee or at the end of a meal, to talk about the business of the day: kids' activities, schedules, household issues, business pressures, upcoming events to plan for, and so on. This is a *must* for the effective oversight of a family and household. Then, once a week if possible, set a time for a longer interchange. This might be a date night when you go out for dinner and talk about the bigger issues of life: dreams, goals, worries, children, and your own relationship. If you can't go out for dinner, at least spend time together in a place off-limits to the family. Do whatever you need to do to set the mood for dialogue: music, wine, hors d'oeuvres, a big blanket—whatever is conducive to honest, caring conversation with the most important person in your life.

Serving:
Being Jesus in day-to-day life

1. *Protect him from outside onslaughts.*
Abigail is an example in the Bible of a woman who took it upon herself to protect her husband (I Samuel 25). As a wife, you are most often the protected one, but there are times when you must be your husband's shield. Do not allow others to speak negatively of him in your presence, insist that your children show him honor in their words and their actions, and make your home a safe haven for him to retreat to every evening after the battles of business he engages in every day.

2. *Find out what pleases him and do it.*
Every man has certain trigger points—the places that will either bring him great joy or great pain. These are the areas in any marriage that can become problematic if ignored. Common areas of sensitivity for men are meals, finances, housekeeping, mental stimulation, and sex. You may already know his standards in each of these (or other) areas. If you know what he wants, find ways to do what he asks. Then seek other ways to go above and beyond what he is asking and do those things, too. Study your partner and know him so well that you anticipate what he would most desire. Pleasing your husband will bring you rewards far in excess of the price you pay for honoring him and his needs.

3. *Serve with faithfulness and love.*
The Bible is full of imperatives concerning faithfulness, not only in marriage, but in our walk with God. Faithfulness is the characteristic

most pleasing to God and, I believe, most needed by our spouses. Your mate needs to know that you will be there no matter what. You will honor your wedding vows without compromise. You will be loyal to the death. But that faithfulness is most effective when it is delivered in love. As much as possible, love your husband as unconditionally as God loves you. Ask God to build that kind of love for him into your very being and then live it out by being a willing servant—following the example of Jesus when he washed his disciples' feet.

Unit Four: God

Devotion:
Relating one-on-one

1. *Giving God the first and the best.*
Someone once said that we should give God the first day of every week, the first ten percent of all we earn, and the first hour of every day. God is the only being in this universe who has the right to say, "Me first." And he does. Before our children, our husbands, our work, and ourselves comes God. Practice that reality by being faithful in spending time with him early in the day before the rest of the world creeps into your consciousness and into your time. Pray, listen, read the Bible, journal your thoughts as you sit quietly and meditatively in his presence. Let the Holy Spirit control you, love you, and direct you. Practicing this daily time alone with God is your way of honoring him as the Lord of your life. When you do that, he promises to bless you: your children, your work, your relationships, your home, and your walk with him. Devotion is a small price to pay for the blessing of the almighty God.

2. *Practicing God's presence throughout the day.*
Once you have made the effort to begin your day with God, take him with you wherever you go. Talk to him as you make breakfast, get your family off to their various places, have coffee with your husband, and head to work. The great contemplatives tell us that it is possible to live life on two levels at once. On one level we are living in this world, interacting with people around us, and accomplishing the tasks in front of us. On a deeper level, our spirits are communing continually with God who is our constant companion. When that begins to happen, you will find yourself talking spontaneously to God about issues that arise and about things that trouble you. You will thank him automatically for the good things that happen. You will have an awareness of the

spiritual in the material and physical all around you, but you will be putting into practice Paul's admonishments to pray always and to take all our anxieties to God.

3. *Keeping short accounts with God.*

The one thing that will keep your relationship with God from maturing is sin. Because Jesus paid the penalty for our sins, we know that when we confess, we will be forgiven. The Holy Spirit convicts us of sin, we confess, God forgives. It's that simple. Your only job in this whole process is confession. Once you confess, which really means that you agree with God that what you have done is sinful, he forgives. You and I can live guilt-free lives. We are free from the penalty of sin and the guiltiness of being sinful beings. Not only that, God has promised to empower us to be free of the bondage to sin. He has overcome the evil one and, therefore, as long as you are dependent upon God, he will overcome sin in our lives. He will help us to recognize it, forgive us when we confess, and give us power to be free to live lives totally devoted to God alone.

Church:
Relating with others who believe

1. *Find a place to get involved.*

God never intended for us to develop as Christians without the support and friendship of other Christians. Early on, the church looked a little different from how it looks today. Groups of believers met together in homes, always on Sunday, but sometime as much as every day of the week. They could not get along without each other. They wanted to relate to others who related to God as they did; they wanted to know God better by knowing his children better. Today the church of our society is more organized. We have scheduled meetings, planned programs, and structured ways of worship. This is not bad, but we must not confuse the church with organized religion. God's definition of "church" is people. His church are all those who know him in a personal way through acceptance of the payment that Jesus made for us on the cross. If that is the biblical definition, we have to admit that many who go to the organized church each Sunday morning are not really part of the church as God defines it. On the other hand, there may be people meeting with their friends at Starbucks and digging together into the Word of God who really are the "church" in the sense that they are God's children seeking God's face together. I say all that to remind you that getting involved in the church may or may not mean putting your name on a membership role. It may be that you find several other people and worship God together in someone's living room. Or it may be that you find the structure of a church organization comfortable and good for your family. In that case, get involved. Go, meet people, relate to others until you find just the right set of believing friends to help you grow up in the family of God.

2. *Learn how to serve other Christians.*

The essence of Jesus's message to those of us who are his followers is that we are to serve. The place that he has designated most clearly for our primary acts of serving is the church. In other words, we are to serve one another. How do we do that? First, there are several passages that describe gifts that the Holy Spirit gives in order to enable us to serve effectively (such as Romans12:4–8 and I Corinthians 12). Those gifts, we are told, are to be used for the building up of the church, those who are part of God's family. Service roles related to those gifts include, among others, teaching, preaching, praying, helping, giving, and showing hospitality. As we begin to identify the gifts God has given us, we begin to see how we can most effectively be of service in the church. The goal of our service is always to build one another up so that we all know God better, present him better to the world around us, and support each other as we develop into the people God wants each of us to be.

3. *Enjoy being served.*

Remember when Jesus got on his knees and washed his disciples' feet? Most of them gratefully allowed him to clean their dusty feet. Peter, though, protested. He knew who Jesus was and he did not want the Son of God washing his feet. Sometimes it is easier for us to serve than to be served. But Jesus taught Peter (and us, too) that accepting another's gift of service is an important part of being a member of the family of God. Sometimes we serve. Sometimes we are the gracious recipients of another's service. When that happens, we simply need to learn to receive with thanksgiving and joy.

Reaching out:
Helping others in Jesus's name

1. *Getting involved in our communities.*
Finding a church where we fit and can grow close to other Christians is critical to our spiritual development, but we have to be careful that we do not get so comfortable there that we forget there are others who still need to be influenced by the truth that we know and the values we live. That influence can best be felt in our world by Christians getting involved in all levels of life in their communities. We can serve on school boards or as school janitors. We can run for City Council or be on the cleanup committee after the parade. We need to vote, to be informed about issues in our communities and in the world, and be able to engage in meaningful conversation about issues that affect us locally and globally. Jesus told his followers that they were the salt of the earth. We know that salt does no good in the saltshaker. It must be spread around in order to have its effect. We sometimes need to reach beyond our comfort zones into a bigger world that greatly needs the influence of level-headed, well informed, and hard-working Christians who are willing to serve both inside and outside the church.

2. *Providing help to those in need.*
At the end of Matthew 25, Jesus makes it very clear that one of the things we will eventually be judged for is how we treated people in need. He goes so far as to say that if we showed kindness to prisoners, strangers, or the hungry, we are showing kindness to him. Jesus identified that strongly with the needy of this world. If we live fairly sheltered lives, we may need to stretch a little to find those who are physically or financially needy. But if our eyes and hearts are open, we will find them. Then

what do we do? First, allow the person to express his need. Sometimes we rush in with help that isn't really the help that is needed. Once a need is expressed, figure out what you can do. Sometimes, giving money is the best way. At other times, we might need to connect a person with a social service agency such as The Salvation Army. Maybe we can provide meals, a temporary place to stay, used clothing (in good condition, of course!), or transportation. Listen, learn, and then do something. Anything we do in response to an expressed need says that we care. We have to get over our fear of being taken advantage of. I agree with trying to follow a path of wisdom, but I would rather have someone receive something from me that they didn't really need than to need something that I could give and not receive it.

3. *Sharing the message that changes lives.*

This is hard for many of us, but there comes a time when we realize that what we have that other people need more than anything else is a relationship with God. Relieving suffering by providing for material needs is very important, but even more important is helping people get connected to the God who can meet the most basic needs of their hearts. How do we do this comfortably? First, I think we get to know someone and meet that person where he or she is at that moment. Then we begin to talk about what God means to us and how we are growing in our relationship with him. As we sense curiosity or questions, we respond. If God has prepared the heart of that individual, the response might be strong enough to cause him or her to accept the great gift of salvation Jesus has offered. If not, we may bring that person to a next level of understanding that someday may lead to the life-changing decision to become a follower of Christ. There is no one right way to share this message. Just about any way will work as long as we are sure of our own standing with God, we share out of a heart of love, and we are sensitive to the responses of the person to whom we are talking. We plant seeds, but God is the only one who can bring a new baby into the family of God.

Unit Five: Body

Fitness:
Building physical strength

1. *Learning to be physical.*
We live in a day of convenience and hurry. As a result, we are required to be less physical than our ancestors had to be. But, if we are savvy in our use of modern conveniences, we can regain some control and gain the benefits of physicality. For example, we can choose to use the stairs instead of the elevator whenever possible. If it is two flights or less, we can almost always beat the elevator in terms of time, anyway. We can park our cars at the far end of the parking lot and hike into the store. It probably won't take us as long as it would take to circle around a couple of times to find the closest possible space. If you like to watch television, find something to do while you watch it that requires some movement: you could lift hand weights, or stand at the counter and sort photographs or work a puzzle. If you have to be on the telephone a lot at home or at work, try standing instead of sitting. Some of the most widely used "road to success" seminars advise that we think better on our feet and, therefore, if we are involved in a conversation that requires us to be sharp mentally, we should be standing even when on the phone. Standing uses more muscles than sitting does and enables us to move around freely. Studies also show that fidgeters use more calories in a day than do people who tend to sit still. Just moving helps our bodies stay fit. Sometimes I think it is a matter of mindset. We can begin by seeing ourselves as energetic, capable, and physical. We can get rid of images that create the need to be pampered and instead can become attuned to using our bodies joyfully and effectively.

2. *Working out for fun and profit.*
Just moving will be a start, but it won't be enough to become physically fit. That will take a little more effort, but the effort will pay big dividends.

Beginning a workout depends on where you are physically right now. The first area to consider, though, is aerobic exercise—something to get the blood pumping through the arteries, something that will encourage your heart muscle to get stronger. Most experts agree that, unless you have physical disabilities, walking is a good way to begin. Other choices include bicycling, walking on a treadmill, stair climbing, jogging, and swimming. The important thing is to find something you enjoy—or can learn to enjoy—and then to stick with it. Most fitness advisers say that you should do an aerobic workout in 35–45-minute segments four or five days a week with the goal being to increase the heart rate [to no more than 80 percent of your maximum heart rate] and keep it at the increased rate for about half an hour.

A second segment of exercise that is particularly important for fitness is weight training. It is important to find a way to work your arm, leg, and back muscles. This builds strength and bone mass, both of which are critical for good health as we age. Pilates and yoga are other types of exercise that help to build muscle and increase flexibility. Instruction in both is available by DVD (more information available at www.winsorpilates.com.) or in classes at local YMCAs or fitness centers. Again, the important things to remember are these:

(a) Start. It's OK to start small, but starting is a must.

(b) Be consistent. Try to do some type of workout every day, alternating with aerobic activity and with weight training or flexibility exercises.

(c) Have fun. This is work, but the satisfaction is great, so stick with it. If it is more fun to work out with a partner, find one. If the social involvement of a class makes it more intriguing, join one. Eventually even the work of fitness becomes fun. Well, kind of.

3. *Balancing life for physical benefit.*
Do you know that one of the biggest health problems of Americans today is lack of sleep? Lack of adequate rest causes undue anxiety, quickness to anger, and susceptibility to disease. We are busy people

and, as a result, we too often do not get enough sleep. God designed us for rest. He gave us a day a week for rest. How many of us really use our Sundays as days of rest? God knows that we function best when we are able to achieve physical rest and we relate best to him when we are able to rest in his presence. Sometimes we just have to slow down, discipline ourselves to turn off the television or give up the project we're working on, and get to bed on time; and we have to slow our minds so that we can rest our hearts in God and sleep soundly. One of the secrets to a healthy life is balance. We balance our diet, our exercise, our schedules, our alone time and social time, our work and our play, our waking and sleeping. We need to allow God to show us what the various balances need to be in our lives at the season we are presently in. His balance for us will be perfect!

Food:
Eating for nutrition and health

1. *Controlling weight.*
There are literally hundreds of books that have been written and published on this topic, so detail here will be unnecessary. As Christians, though, it is important that we get the concept of weight control in the heavenly perspective. If we are significantly overweight, we may diminish our effectiveness in drawing others into relationship with God. If we are obsessed with weight control or caught up in overindulgence, we are not reflecting the balanced life we discussed above. If weight, appearance, or food becomes a focus for us, God has taken a secondary position. But if there are changes we need to make, evidence is there that small steps over a long period of time are more effective in weight management than more radical dieting or exercise regimens. If we can think of one thing today that we can do to improve the way we eat and implement that one thing, then we are moving in the right direction. Maybe a few days later, we think of one more thing. When that habit becomes ingrained, another is easy to add. For example, maybe today we change our evening ice cream treat to fat-free frozen yogurt instead. Or we have one cookie for dessert instead of two. Then, next week, we may find that we can get by without dessert at all a couple of evenings

a week. Maybe we decide to walk around the yard before dinner this week. Then a few days later, we find that we want new scenery and we walk around the block. Before long, one block becomes two, our habits become healthier, and unwanted pounds melt away. One step at a time. One small change today yields long-term benefit.

2. *Paying attention to nutritional value.*

We have all heard the maxim, "You are what you eat." Our overall health is a combination of many things, including lifestyle, exercise, and genetic makeup. However, choices about what we eat have a significant effect on the quality of our lives. Learn to read labels to determine what you are eating in terms of calories, fat, and nutrition. If you are dealing with a health issue, find out what nutritionists say about foods or certain vitamins that may enable the body to deal effectively with that problem. Go to the websites of your favorite fast food restaurants to read the nutritional values of their offerings. Then choose two or three from every site that you find acceptable nutritionally. When you to go Arby's or Taco Bell or Burger King, you will already have in your mind an idea of what you will or will not order. That way, you will protect yourself from loading up on unwanted cholesterol or calories. Read, read, read. There are books, health magazines readily available for our self-education. We need to take advantage of these resources and become our own best friend in making good nutritional choices.

3. *Enjoying God's bounty.*

In our culture, we have found ways to "improve" on what God has created for us to eat. We use oleomargarine when God gave us butter. We dip apples in caramel to make them taste sweeter. We salt and pickle and fry and baste until the natural tastes that God has built in are buried under our artificial concoctions. The rule of thumb is to eat foods as close to the way God made them as possible. Eat raw fruits and vegetables at least some of the time. Eat some things without sauces, butters, or spices just to enjoy the flavor that God built in. And then, what you do eat, enjoy! Be thankful to the God who has given us abundant food and myriad choices and relish each bite. Chew thoroughly, taste completely, and swallow with thanksgiving. Food is our sustenance, to be sure, but it is also a source of enjoyment. Eat what you need or desire, share what you have with others, and enjoy the pleasures of good, God-given food.

Beauty:
Promoting what God has given

1. *Putting your best face forward.*
We do have some tools to make ourselves look as good as possible. These include cleansing and moisturizing products that help to take good care of the skin that God has provided and cosmetic products that help to hide some flaws and to enhance our mouths, eyes, and facial contours. If we take a little time to find out about what works and does not work for us, we will make good use of these resources and face the world with confidence, knowing that we have done all we can to present ourselves in the best possible light. The first step is to take inventory of what you have and what you may need in terms of products. You should have an effective cleanser and good moisturizer (if you can afford it, one for daytime with sun protection and one for nighttime for heavier application). Then you need a concealer for undereye circles and any blemishes you may need to cover, a foundation, some eye shadow (optional), cheek color, mascara, and lip color. That's it. You don't need a whole drawerful of makeup, so get busy and throw out the outdated bottles and applicators. Save only the most current colors and products. For a real treat, you could go to a salon and ask for some advice about the colors and products that are right for your skin condition and tones. A cheaper way to get similar advice is to go to a friend who sells products such as BeautiControl or Mary Kay and ask them to advise you. Stay current on colors and trends by picking up a women's magazine now and then. There is a beauty/cosmetics article in almost every issue.

2. *Dressing for success.*
Ever since the fall in the Garden of Eden, clothes have been important. There are huge industries in fashion, manufacture, sales, and resales

that prove that point. We all look pretty much alike when we are naked. Our individuality is expressed in what we choose to wear. So, we must choose carefully! Make sure you have a few classic pieces in your wardrobe: tailored slacks, a good suit, the little black dress, and well fitting jeans. Choose a few good quality pairs of shoes and other accessories such as handbags and jewelry to go with these basics. After that, you can expand your wardrobe based on your personal taste and, of course, budget. Make sure that for each season, you have something that is quality and current. Keep everything mended, clean, and pressed so that on a moment's notice you can put together an outfit for almost any occasion. Then, keep your closet cleaned out. At the beginning of every season, cull through what you no longer wear and give it to The Salvation Army or Goodwill. Let someone else get use out of what is no longer useful to you. That way, you will know that what is in your closet is ready to wear, is current in style, and is something you like.

3. Encouraging the eye of the beholder.
There are two things we can do to make others see us as beautiful even if we are not runway models. The first is to smile. One of the most beautiful things you can wear is a smile. When you smile, you invite others into your world and you make yourself welcome into theirs. Facial and bodily faults disappear when you smile. Your eyes light up and draw attention from the age-related wrinkles to the joy-related crinkles. Smiling will cause others to perceive you as beautiful. The second thing we can do to encourage others to see us in a favorable light is to be interested in them. The less we are focused on ourselves and what we look like, the more we are able to be concerned about and interested in other people. The folks we talk to will see us as friendly and beautiful if we treat them as if they are important and worth our time and attention. It's true. Others look at us more positively if they feel good about themselves when they are talking to us. If beauty is in the eye of the beholder, we can give the beholder's eye slightly blurred vision when it comes to our physical faults by smiling and by being interested in them as a dearly loved creation of God.

Unit Six: Development

Assessment:
Figuring out where you are

1. *Journal to find out what you are thinking.*
Do some self-assessment by engaging in thought-provoking exercises to evaluate who you are, what you want to accomplish in your life, what your strengths and weaknesses are, and what brings you satisfaction. Exercises could include such things as listing your top five talents, your top ten areas of interest, your most rewarding relationships, memories of accomplishments that brought you pleasure, and so forth. Write about what you like to do when you have a few hours or a day to spend in any way you choose. List the last five books you have read and write about why you chose each, what you liked or did not like about each, and what you may have learned about yourself from each. Look at goals you have written and write about where you are in achieving each of them. Are there any you need to change? Are there any you need to add? Make a list of obstacles you see in reaching particular goals.

You may think of other exercises that will assist you in evaluating who you are and what direction you desire to move in. This series of exercises will help to ensure that the path you choose will come out of the deepest desires, abilities, and needs of your heart and not out of any outside pressures. You need to become all that God created you to be, but before you are able to do that, you need to assess where you are right now. All of these writings should be done in an attitude of prayer and of listening for God's guidance in the self-evaluation process.

2. *Use available assessment vehicles.*
There are many books on discovering strengths, identifying values, and formulating goals and are readily accessible if you browse at your local bookstore or library. Some of these books will include self-assessment tests and questionnaires that will guide your thinking as you focus on

life's purpose. In addition, many colleges have placement offices that will assist in assessing abilities and interests. If all else fails, find a good psychologist or career counselor who will (for a fee, of course) conduct a series of personality profiles in an effort to find what kind of work or activity is fulfilling and vitalizing to you. If you have been used to doing for most of your life what others have expected of you, you may need help in digging through the top layers of your life to find the real you underneath. These assessments will be of great help in getting to the truth of who you are and what kind of hobby or work (volunteer or paid) would bring you the most satisfaction.

3. Write a mission statement for your life.

Traditionally, a mission statement should be only once sentence long. It should simply state what you are living for. Why are you here? What is your life all about? Someone once said that every person has his hour. Out of your whole life, if you had only one hour in which to do something significant or something that would affect others or change the world you touch, what would it be? The answer to that question will help you zero in on your life's mission. Write it down and you have your mission statement. Memorize it. Live by it. Remind yourself of it daily. Then, by God's grace, you will begin to live it out. You never know when it will be your hour.

Training:
Learning what you need to know

1. Check into education opportunities.

If you look at your mission statement and realize that your goals are loftier than your present skills will allow you to reach, you may need to get more training. One way to do that is through formal education. Our culture is so open to second careers that many of the students sitting in college classrooms today are older adults. Check into degree programs or class-by-class opportunities to expand your understanding and/or credentials in the area to which you aspire. It may be that seminars or talent-specific training such as art classes, public speaking, or psychology will be all that you need if a degree is not essential to achieving your goals. Order catalogs from colleges in your area or check out course offerings on-line. Allow yourself to get caught up in the possibilities that formal education could open up for you.

2. Find out how you can teach yourself.
As the writer of Ecclesiastes said, "Of making many books there is no end ..." (12:12b). For those of us who are lifelong learners, that is a very good thing. If you want to learn, go find some good books and start reading. If you do a bit of research, you can also find correspondence courses and lectures on just about any subject on tape or CD. If there is a topic you want to get smarter about, there is probably someone willing to sell you a way to learn it. The Internet is a great search tool for finding these resources. Amazon.com seems to have it all! Read, study, learn, practice and you will grow in understanding and authority in taking yourself a step closer to living a life of meaning and purpose.

3. Find someone else who can teach you.
If you want to learn flower arranging, find the very best designer you know and ask if she will teach you. You will have to pay for this, of course (unless he or she is a very good friend!), but one-on-one learning is sometimes the most efficient in moving you along the path to excellence. You may be able to find a job as an apprentice in an area in which you have interest. On-the-job training has been around as long as people have. If your goals are broader than learning specific tasks, find someone who seems to know how to do what it is you want to do and ask them to guide you. Don't be afraid to ask. Most people are flattered that you admire and aspire to what they know or what they do well. Even if they turn you down, they will feel good about your asking.

Experience:
Growing through the world around you

1. Start at home.

Whatever your life's goals are, your family is a logical place to start to put them into practice. Include your family in your plans and begin to work out your mission statement on your spouse, your children, your parents, and your siblings. It is hard to conceive of *any* mission statement that would not have application to those who are closest to you. Put it into practice. Talk about it with those in your family who are mature enough to give you feedback or open enough to learn from your example. It is both safest and hardest to begin to live out your life's mission at home. These are the people who love you most, but who also know you best. There is no better testing ground for the level of your commitment to the goals you have set. There is no safer place to discover that the mission (or the way you get there) may have to be revised.

2. *Reach out to your friends.*

Since your mission statement will uncover the core of who you are, it will go beyond your world of work or service and will encompass all relationships. Include your friends in your vision, either by practicing it on them or by asking for their feedback, ideas, and support. Friends like to see you grow and develop. They will be encouragers and, hopefully, will be honest in their responses to your inquiries and supportive of your efforts.

3. *Find places of service.*

Whatever your mission, there is undoubtedly someone or some organization out there who needs the kind of thing you want to accomplish. See if you can find a place to put your mission to work—at a church, school, a hospital or nursing home, a youth organization, a social service agency, or another place that relies upon volunteers. There is no better way to test the validity of your mission than to put it to work in the neediest of places. You will find nourishment for your soul and inspiration for your journey as you seek the place where what you give will have the most significant impact. Don't volunteer just anywhere, though. Make sure the organization you serve shares your fundamental values and goals and that the job they give you enables you to test the validity of your mission and your readiness to live it out.

BIBLIOGRAPHY

Andrew, Brother, with John and Elizabeth Sherrill. *God's Smuggler.* Grand Rapids, Michigan: Chosen Books, a division of Baker House Company, 2001.

Cunningham, Loren, with Janice Rogers. *Is That Really You, God?* Grand Rapids, Michigan: Chosen Books, a division of The Zondervan Publishing House, 1984.

Dowis, Richard. *The Lost Art of the Great Speech.* New York, New York: MJF Books, a division of American Management Association, 2000.

Guinness, Os. *The Call.* Nashville, Tennessee: Word Publishing, Inc., 1998.

Hendricks, Howard. *Teaching to Change Lives.* Sisters, Oregon: Multnomah Publishers, Inc., 1987.

Jacobi, Jeffrey. *How to Say It with Your Voice.* Paramus, New Jersey: Prentice Hall, Inc., 1996.

Kierkegaard, Soren. *Provocations.* Robertsbridge, East Sussex, Tennessee: The Plough Publishing House of The Bruderhof Foundation, Inc., 2002.

Lawson, James Gilchrist. *Deeper Experiences of Famous Christians.* Uhrichsville, Ohio: Barbour Publishing, Inc., 2000.

Lewis, C. S. *Poems.* New York, New York: Harcourt Brace Jovanovich, Publishers, 1964.

Mancur, Michael, *Quotations Page,* www.quotationspage.com, 1994-2005.

Manning, Brennan. *The Ragamuffin Gospel.* Sisters, Oregon: Multnomah Publishers, Inc., 2000.

Manning, Brennan. *Ruthless Trust.* New York, New York: HarperCollins Publishers, Inc., 2000.

McKenzie, E.C. *14,000 Quips and Quotes.* Peabody, Massachusetts: Hendrickson Publishers, Inc. under arrangement with Baker Book House Company, 1980.

Miller, Donald. *Blue Like Jazz*. Nashville, Tennessee: Thomas Nelson, Inc., 2003.

Richardson, Michael. *Amazing Faith*. Colorado Springs, Colorado: WaterBrook Press, a division of Random House, Inc., 2000.

Tournier, Paul. *A Listening Ear*. Minneapolis, Minnesota: Augsberg Publishing House, 1987.

Yun, Brother with Paul Hattaway. *The Heavenly Man*. London, England: Monarch Books in conjunction with Christian Solidarity Worldwide, 2002.

About the Author

Beverly Van Kampen is a freelance writer, Bible teacher, and speaker. In addition to writing magazine articles and Bible studies, she serves as a writer of supportive study materials for seminary level coursework for the Institute of Theological Studies in Grand Rapids, Michigan, and is the author of *The GodSense Devotional* (FaithWalk Publishing 2004).

A former journalist, she has a degree in both journalism and education from Central Michigan University having taken two years of undergraduate coursework at Taylor University in Upland, Indiana and graduate work in communications at Western Michigan University. She taught high school and middle school English for several years, two of which were at an English-speaking school in Honduras, Central America.

She also served for a time as Managing Director of *The Scriptorium: Center for Christian Antiquities*. *The Scriptorium*, now located in Orlando, Florida, houses a large collection of ancient Christian manuscripts and early printed editions of the Bible and related documents, which are made available for scholarly research and for guided viewing by the public.

As vice president of Investment Property Associates, Inc. of Grand Haven, Van Kampen had a successful career in various roles related to the development of investment real estate throughout western Michigan.

She lives in Spring Lake, Michigan with her husband, Warren, a retired physician. They have four grown children and three grandsons. She can be contacted via her website at www.beverlyvankampen.com.